Can't Ruffle This Feather

A single women's journey around the world in order to discover who God created her to be

Angela M. Bushi

WESTBOW
PRESS
A DIVISION OF THOMAS NELSON

WestBow Press books may be ordered through booksellers or by contacting:

WestBow Press
A Division of Thomas Nelson
1663 Liberty Drive
Bloomington, IN 47403
www.westbowpress.com
1-(866) 928-1240

ISBN: 978-1-4497-2580-8 (sc)
ISBN: 978-1-4497-2581-5 (hc)
ISBN: 978-1-4497-2579-2 (e)

Library of Congress Control Number: 2011915515

Printed in the United States of America

WestBow Press rev. date: 10/18/2011

My mom and dad for giving me wings,
Nonna for all her love,
Justin, who loved life,
Lucas for having rock solid faith,
and David—my answer to prayer!

Now unto him that is able to do exceeding abundantly
above all that we ask or think, according to the power
that worketh in us.

Ephesians 3:20

American Standard Version

CONTENTS

FOREWORD

One of my favorite characters in Scripture is Simeon. Simeon is only mentioned briefly in Luke, chapter two, but he was given a wonderful gift. Simeon was described as a devout and righteous man who had been told by the Holy Spirit that he would get to see the Messiah before he died.

I can't imagine how this man felt when it was revealed to him that he, among all the people of Israel, would be given the privilege of seeing the long-awaited Messiah. Depending on which translation of the Bible you read, it says that one day Simeon was led, prompted, moved, or guided by the Holy Spirit to go to the temple in Jerusalem. It was there that Simeon was given not only the privilege of seeing Jesus, but also the chance to hold the Messiah, his Savior, his King. Because he was obedient to the leading of the Spirit, Simeon was given an incredible gift: he saw Jesus.

In many ways, Angie Feather Bushi reminds me of Simeon. She will blush when we say this, but she is a devout and righteous woman, one who listens to the Holy Spirit. Not only does she listen, she is obedient to what He says to her, even if she doesn't quite understand His sovereign perspective. Because she listened and obeyed, she has been given some wonderful gifts. These gifts include some incredible adventures as she has followed the lead of Jesus. Who would go to Bulgaria as a young single woman unless the Lord told her to? Then to Switzerland, the Philippines, inner-city San Francisco, Denver, and now Detroit? Every time she was obedient to do what the Lord asked her to do, she got to see Jesus. She saw Jesus in the people and the events of her life. She saw Jesus in places and in ways she never dreamed that she would see Him. All because she was led, prompted, moved, and guided, by the Holy Spirit and was obedient.

We know that as you read this book, you will have an opportunity to see Jesus, maybe in a new way. The book may help you hear His voice as He speaks to you, and it may inspire you to try something new. Because whenever we are led by the Spirit, as Simeon and Angie have been, He always takes us to Jesus.

JC Bowman   Barb Bowman

Young Life Idaho Regional Director   V.P. Ministry Advancement
                                 Mission Aviation Fellowship

CHAPTER 1

Everything I Touch Turns to Gold

Every teenager longs to be recognized and accepted. We all establish an identity, whether we like it or not, and expectations are placed on us according to that identity. I was lucky: my identity was that of a good student and an exceptional athlete. In high school, I played golf on the boys' team and shot in the mid seventies. I played on the varsity tennis team from my freshman year on and went to the state tournament each year. My high school career culminated in a basketball state championship, where I was voted first team all-state. I had a great group of friends known as the "proud crowd," and I was voted prom queen my senior year. In addition to all of that, I was an honor student.

Life was great, and I loved every minute of it—or so it appeared. However, like many teenage girls, when no one was looking, I struggled with my body image and weight and I tried to please everyone. Then, during winter break of my sophomore year of high school, my entire world was rocked. My older brother, Justin, was ice skating in Breckenridge, Colorado, when he fell and hit his head. He had a severe seizure and was airlifted by helicopter to a hospital in Denver. When the doctors examined him, I heard those words that everyone prays they never hear: "Your brother has cancer." Justin was diagnosed with a malignant brain tumor and given between three and six months to live. He immediately underwent surgery and radiation. Justin was full of faith and confidence and some of that teenage "nothing-bad-will-happen-to-me" mentality. He insisted that I play in my basketball game in Durango, Colorado, instead of attending his surgery. He was very adamant about this, so we compromised: I waited to see him come out of surgery and then hopped on a private plane to Durango, where my team was playing basketball. The busier I kept myself, the less I had to think about things. I became more selfish than I already was and began to put a protective covering around my heart so it wouldn't hurt as much.

This could not be happening to me—everything I did turned to gold! I had no coping mechanism for dealing with the idea of losing my brother to cancer. I started to drink, skipped classes to play tennis, and just stopped caring. I had grown up in an Episcopal church but now decided that there must not be a god. Justin was the kindest, happiest person I knew and if something like this could happen to him . . . then there must not be a god. Little did I know that—just as God promises in Psalms—he heard my cries and had captured my tears in a bottle. He sent this young couple, JC and Barb Bowman, and they moved in next door. They started reaching out to me. They would invite me over for dinner or takeout pizza, they attended my sporting events, and they shared sincere concern for my feelings and despair. They were heading up a ministry for teenagers called Young Life and even though I wasn't interested in that, I felt that they genuinely cared about me so I hung out with them a lot.

That summer following Justin's diagnosis and surgery, JC and Barb invited me to go with them to a camp in Minnesota. I jumped at a chance to get away from home and the stress that was everywhere there. It was there that I heard about the love of God and that He wanted a personal relationship with me. On June 17, 1987, I asked Christ into my heart. I will never forget that long bus ride back to Colorado and how I just stared straight ahead with a silly grin on my face. That void in my heart was full of His light and all I could do was smile. Becoming a Christian gave me new hope and a source of strength to draw from, but a new guilt set in. "Why, God? Did you give Justin cancer just in order for me to believe you in?" Why couldn't I just believe by hearing the word like so many people? Why did it take such a catastrophic event for me to believe?" Becoming a Christian made me a nicer person and I stopped those destructive behaviors, but deep down inside, I still longed to figure out who I really was.

The summer after my graduation, I was on Young Life's work crew in Ramona, California. I spent my days raking a patch of dead grass the size of a football field under the hot sun. I remember so clearly how uneasiness grew inside of me. With so many worldly accomplishments and such a bright future, I was the envy of many people. I was the "total package." I was athletic, smart, and such a good Christian. I even received a college basketball scholarship to the University of Northern Colorado. Oh, how easy it is to get labeled one thing and to have that thing becomes your identity. But now I wasn't sure the label fit.

Who Am I Really?

I wasn't happy with who I was. I knew that something was missing from me being able to enjoy that abundant life that God promises. "The thief comes only to steal and kill and destroy; I have come that they may have life, and have it to the full" (John 10:10). I thought that college would be my chance to for a fresh start. No longer did I have to be Angie Feather, the athlete, or Angie, the church girl, or Angie, the one who makes no mistakes, or Angie, the girl who pleases everyone. This was my chance to become Angie the uh . . . or Angie the one who . . . That was just it. *That* was my problem. I didn't know who I wanted to be—I just knew it wasn't who I had been.

I ended up quitting basketball and giving up my scholarship. I was heartbroken. But God uses all things for the good for those who love Him. I began coaching high school basketball and decided to start a Young Life club in my college town. I changed my major from pre-physical therapy to secondary science education and became involved in Campus Crusade for Christ. I didn't really date much in college, but since I was about to graduate, it was time to start looking for my husband, right? My senior year, I did date a boy who lived in Wisconsin, so I was "dating," but it was not serious since it was long distance. I found this to become a pattern in my life—I term it the "safe" date—where I had no worries about anything getting too serious. College was great—I had a lot of friends, was involved in many activities, and graduated in four and a half years, and was debt-free thanks to my dad. One thing college did teach me was that sports did not fill the hole in my heart.

The great news was that God had performed a miracle and Justin's tumor was gone. He had been going in every couple of months for MRI scans to monitor his tumor because they could not get all of it out during the surgery. One day the MRI scanned showed that the tumor was completely gone. The doctors could not explain it. It wasn't until then, almost six years after his initial diagnosis, that I realized it was not my fault. God did not give him cancer so I would believe in Him, but He did use his cancer to reach me and many others in my family.

A key event happened the summer after I graduated and I should have seen this as foreshadowing to what was to come. It involved the man I met the summer before at Young Life camp, the one I had been dating long distance while I was in Colorado and he was in Wisconsin. I remember walking hand in hand by a lake and discussing our future as we watched the sun set. I knew that this was the man I was going to spend the rest of my life with. But when I woke up the next morning, my feelings toward him were completely gone. In fact, I didn't even care to see him again. I tried to fight what I thought was fear and asked God to take it away. The feeling, however, was growing stronger—this was not the man for me. So we broke up. It wasn't until a month later that I realized why God wanted me single for right now—so I would hear His call on my life.

My first job out of college was back in my old hometown of Grand Junction, Colorado. I was hired to teach eighth-grade science at the new middle school. Life seemed good, but was it really? I could see myself teaching at this great school, in this great Colorado town for the rest of my life—and that scared me to death. *There has to be more to life than this!* I thought. I began training for a marathon with American Cancer Society's Team in Training and that gave me hours of pounding the pavement to think and pray. My goal was to raise money for the American Cancer Society and run the San Francisco Marathon. Since graduating from college and moving home, I had lost my Christian support group and church, Bible study, and prayer became less important. Once again, I found myself falling back into the mindset where athletic achievements and people-pleasing dominated me. Once again, I was having an identity crisis.

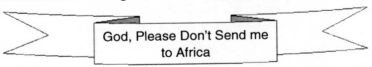

God, Please Don't Send me
to Africa

If you have ever run a marathon, you know what tricks your mind can play during those 26.2 miles. As I ran up and down and up and down the hills of San Francisco for over four hours, God began to work on my heart. I think it was mile seventeen when I turned a corner and was hit by a thirty-mile-per-hour wind right in the face as I ran along the Embarcadero along the bay. I actually stopped because of the pain and cried out to God. I pleaded with Him to take me now—and I meant it! I was in so much pain, and stopping didn't help, so I kept running—no . . . jogging slowly. It was then that God said He had plans for me, to give me a hope and a future. And I knew that He was asking me to leave my comfort zone of sports and teaching and Colorado and move overseas. I had a crisis of faith when Justin was sick, a crisis of identity in school, and now I was having a crisis of the comfort zone. I had to go wherever God was asking me to go. The verse He put in my heart was Romans 1:16: "I am not ashamed of the gospel because it is the power of God for the salvation of everyone who believes."

The day I got back from San Francisco (to my parents' house where I was once again living) I called Young Life to see what they had overseas. (There was no Internet yet.) I thought I could teach English or something along those lines. When I called, they told me about a ministry they had of sending teachers to these international schools to teach and lead a Young Life Club. This was a perfect fit for me, and I decided to do it. One of my traits that I have not yet mentioned is my ability to be super stubborn; once my mind is made up, no one can change it. This was one of those situations where my mind was made up. And for some reason, only God knows why, this small-town girl living the perfect life felt compelled to move halfway around the world. I needed an adventure, and this was my opportunity. Little did I know that the decision I made that day is one that would take me around all the way around the world. The ironic thing was that two different times in college, I had applied to go on an exchange program to Oxford, England—and both times, the moment I learned I had been accepted, I chickened out, too afraid to leave the United States.

Next thing I know, I am driving to Young Life's headquarters in Colorado Springs, Colorado, for a two-week training course. Initially, it was said that I would be going to Spain. Boy, God is great. I was so excited about this placement that I purchased my ticket with the money I saved up. I started listening to all the Spanish language tapes I could find and wished I had paid more attention to my Spanish classes in high school and college. However, there was a family in Eastern Europe who had been pleading with Young Life to send a staff person there, so the next thing I knew, I was going to Bulgaria. I was a bit disappointed, as I had been studying Spanish and had done a lot of research about the country. Spain is a first world country, and my safety was not a concern there. But I was young, naïve, and adventurous. As long as it wasn't Africa, I was okay with Bulgaria. At first, I actually thought it was somewhere in Central or South America. I came to find out it sits just above Greece and Turkey, west of Macedonia, and below Romania.

In preparation for my mission, we took a family picture, just in case I didn't return. I had radial keratotomy (RK), the archaic form of Lasik surgery; it's an incision made with a precision-calibrated diamond knife. I didn't know if they would have contact lens solution there. My parents didn't say much about me going to such a remote, recently communist country. Probably because they knew that I was going to do what I wanted to do, whether the liked it or not. I was fortunate to train with so many wonderful couples there in Colorado Springs who were also going to be ministering around the world. It was a great time of fellowship and encouragement, and I took pride in the fact that I was going alone and didn't need a husband or partner.

I learned that I would be involved in Young Life's ministry called International School ministry. I would be targeting the kids who are termed *Third Culture Kids* (abbreviated TCKs). Young Life uses this term when referring "to someone who [as a child] has spent a significant period of time in one or more culture(s) other than his or her own, thus integrating elements of those cultures and their own birth culture, into a third culture." So, even though I would be living in Bulgaria, my students would be kids from all over the world who now lived in Bulgaria and spoke English, mostly kids of diplomats and international businessmen. The idea behind this was that these children were left out of the typical missionary focus. The TCK builds relationships to all of the cultures, while not having full ownership of any. Although elements from each culture are assimilated into the TCK's life experience, we worked to build that missing sense of belonging and being in relationships with others of a similar background. These kids can be very transient, moving from country to country, which makes it even more difficult to build relationships with them in order to share the gospel.

I decided I would give God two years of my life, get this missionary bug out of my system, and then return to my safe job in my safe town where I was, well, safe. I put my heart on hold and trusted that God would bring "the man" into my life, perhaps even in Bulgaria. I was sitting outside taking in the sun while reading up on Bulgaria when the words sung by Steven Curtis Chapman, "Waiting for Lightning" struck deep to my soul: "Waiting for lightning, a sign that it's time for a change, and you're listening for thunder, while He quietly whispers your name." I was waiting for God to do something big to speak to me—and he had been calling my name.

CHAPTER 2

Where in the World Is Bulgaria?

I will never in my lifetime forget the flight to Bulgaria as I, a very naive twenty-three-year-old, landed in former communist Sophia, Bulgaria, for an adventure far beyond what I had signed up for. This is how God tends to work in my life—I just sort of blindly go where He says, without really doing a thorough assessment of the situation. I arrived at night, and as we neared the airport, it looked as if the city was on fire; to this day, I still do not know why there were so many fires. My eyes stung from all the cigarette smoke on that Balkan Airlines flight. Back then, smoking was permitted on flights—and by my estimation, I was the only nonsmoker on the flight. The smell of the bodies that needed deodorant mixed with that of the cold cuts, which had no refrigeration, and the cigarette smoke, made me nauseated upon landing.

As I got off the plane, I was greeted by hundreds of people holding posters of pictures of who I thought to be the president of Bulgaria—only to learn later that it was their beloved Hristo Stoichkov, a world-class soccer player. Steve and Marta Gillilan, two teachers from the Anglo-American School of Sophia, were there to pick me up. They had just finished one year in Bulgaria already and proved to be a godsend to me. I was going to live with them until I could find a place of my own. They greeted me with the great news that the PE teacher had resigned and the school needed a teacher.

Even though I was not credentialed in this area, I had experience with PE and sports and could surely teach PE to the fifth to eighth graders. This was a total God thing. I didn't know how I was going to get my work visa so I could stay in the country, and yet, God provided a way. Even more, the job provided a good income, so I only had to raise ministry expenses and not living expenses.

My initial impression of Bulgaria was that it was a dull place. All the people wore black, the buildings were all gray, and the vegetation was all dead. The air felt like pure exhaust from all the public buses giving off so much pollution. Each night when I blew my nose, grey gunk would come out. I decided to keep a detailed journal during my time in Bulgaria, so that I could have an outlet for my thoughts and feelings and also so that I would have the events of the year documented. Journaling has become a valuable part of my mental health throughout my time overseas and the deep inner tender thoughts of an independent, strong woman are honestly expressed in them.

Sept. 19, 1994

My first day in Sofia. I was greeted by the VanderWeeles, Marta and Steve. Very nice, friendly people. Their dreams are high, and I like that. They are looking for me to tell them what to do and when to do it.

The Lord is so amazing. Yesterday, the PE teacher quit, so there is a teaching opening. Praise God. He is faithful.

Today all of the hot water in Sofia has been turned off for three weeks. So, it looks like I will be bathing far and few in-between. I have so much to plan for the upcoming days, but I must make more time to be with the Lord.

Sept. 21, 1994

> *Met the Coxes who head up the Navigators here. Saw a man walking his bear down the street! Actually got on the bus with me!*

> *The parents of this "youth group" are very nice, but have their own ideas of what it looks like and should be like. I am going to have to be bold and tell them how I would like things done instead. Changed my first Leva today and learned how to count to ten. All of my physical and social needs are being met.*

> *I must spend more time with God!*

One of the most challenging obstacles that I faced initially was, of course, the language barriers: verbal and written. Bulgarian is written in the Cyrillic alphabet and is very similar to Russian in that way. In fact, it was actually two Bulgarians Methodist and Cyrillic who developed the alphabet, not the Russians. Theirs is a small country that is not credited with much except creating the alphabet. This accomplishment is even honored with a national holiday.

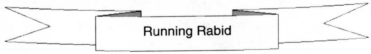

Running Rabid

As I started settling into the daily life here in Bulgaria, I realized how blessed we are in the United States. Since communism had recently fallen and the people now had a choice as to how to spend their money, there was great poverty. Before the fall of communism, all their basic needs—food, water, and electricity—were provided for them by the government. There was no dispensable income to have to decide how to spend. Now, everything had changed with the new government and new found financial freedoms. This caused big problems in budgeting. Food was very sparse, and they also struggled with great inflation. One of the first things I learned was that if you saw some food you wanted, you had to buy it that moment—for tomorrow, it would be gone. There were no grocery stores, but just food kiosks that were there one day and gone the next. I came to love *"shopska"* salad, which is a combination of cucumbers and tomatoes. We had this at every meal. Marta and I also learned to make our own tortillas out of flour and water. In addition to the lack of food, there happened to be a drought in the country that year, so the water was turned off regularly. Every third day, they would turn it on for a few hours. So if you heard the water turn on and you were at work or shopping, you had to rush home and fill up your containers to store up for the dry days. Imagine how disgusting the bathrooms at school were as the toilets filled up and the hot air increased the fermentation process.

There were so many rabid dogs running around that we actually had to use high-pitched dog whistles to keep them at bay. Every recess and at the end of the day, we would have to blow the whistle so the kids could safely go outside. The scary things was that some dogs were so sick, they were unaffected by the whistle. One day a new friend of mine named Howe, a Christian who was here teaching a business class at Sophia University, was bitten by one of these dogs. He went to our embassy to get the series of rabies shots, yet he was denied the shots since he was not embassy personnel. This proved to be a very poor move on the part of the Americans, because Howe was engaged to the daughter of a senator—and this man did not hesitate to call the ambassador on his future son-in-law's behalf, to let the him know of his wrongdoings to fellow Americans. He was fortunate that the British Embassy had the shots and gladly administered them to him.

Sept. 23, 1994

Every day I am learning more and more about the history of Bulgaria. It helps me to understand why people are so passive.

My heart hurts for the international kids; they are so lonely and sheltered. Please, Lord, help me to love and embrace all of these children. Every child I have talked to remarked about how they wished they had lived or could live in one place for a while. I want them to come to know that Jesus will always be with them and will not move away.

Sept. 25, 1994

Had a wonderful picnic tonight. There were probably forty people there. They are really expecting miraculous things from me. I am feeling insufficient. Only the Lord can do this job. So I must allow Him to work through me. As people look to me for leadership, I pray for guidance. Help me to delegate.

I have felt so welcome by all the Christian families. Having dinner and hanging out has been wonderful. Thank You, Lord, for all the support that I am greeted with.

Sept. 27, 1997

The first Wyld Life (middle school) club was tonight. The Lord blessed us by bringing nine kids. There was a lot of enthusiasm and excitement here. Thank You for Myles and his excitement to bring non-Christian friends.

Lord, continue to work in the group and help it to not become stagnant.

Talked to Jim and Beanie at Young Life HQ for the first time since I've been here. Got some business stuff accomplished, and it was nice to hear from them. I am looking forward to our conference in November. I pray that the finances will continue to be enough to enable me to go.

Lord, thank You for all of the open arms that You have surrounded me with. Thank You for the open door now at the American College of Sophia, which is where the international kids go to high school.

Greece, My Refuge

In order to combat the food situation, we would go to Greece once a month and sneak food back across the border. Thankfully, the Gillilans had a car and they offered to take me each time they went. It was such a breath of fresh air to be in such a beautiful country, where they had a McDonald's that even served beer.

Sept. 29, 1994

I am amazed each day to learn how helpless this nation feels. Today the board of directors denied my application as a full-time teacher because of my Christian affiliation. They are afraid of what the Bulgarian government would do to the school if my beliefs were uncovered. So it leaves me with a few options, but I am going to ask for a revote and talk to the board.

I think the fact that the job fell through, I still haven't found an apartment, and I felt a little lonely today has cause the honeymoon period to be over. The reality of where this country stands has hit me. Everything is run down and dirty. People have no sense of personal hygiene, and there is pornography everywhere. At times, many times, I feel like everything I touch is dirty.

Marta and Steve continue to be a bright spot in my life. Marta and I get along very well. Thank God for them.

Oct. 2, 1994

We had our first high school club tonight. Things went well. I thank God for the eight kids that were there. I had dinner with the VanderWeeles, who have been great.

Satan is trying very hard to keep Christians out of Bulgaria. Lord, I pray that we would not be so boastful about the fact that we are being "persecuted" for Jesus. You love a humble heart.

My prayers are that I would continue to meet new people and make new friendships. Lord, please place those hearts in my path that are ready to hear about Your love.

There were things that I observed that made no sense to me. Each major intersection houses checkpoint towers where guards sit and record the coming and going of everyone. Yet since the fall of communism, there was no one to report to, but it was their job—so they continued to sit there. It was also common practice not to talk on the public buses, because when communism ruled, this was not permitted. There were long lines of women waiting for bread, and I learned to do the same. When I wanted water, I had to walk into the woods to a local well. I began to feel like I could make it here, as I am fending for myself, finding food and water. I actually fell in love with a local pastry called *banitza,* filled with feta cheese and then fried. Thankfully, I had started running again, because my diet was anything but healthy. Yet even when I ran, I had to use the dog whistle to keep the rabid dogs away. I was very thankful for the dog whistle.

Oct. 3, 1994

I had my first Bulgarian lesson and first day of class. Both were fun and went well. The Lord was gracious today and was alive inside my heart. It felt wonderful. The business has picked up and feels good as well.

I pray that as I have more and more to do that I would spend more time with the Lord. I never spend enough time with Him. I wish I could live in unceasing prayer.

My days of loneliness have gone quickly, praise God. I still pray for a good single friend. Lord, I lift that up to You.

Oct. 10, 1994

I had a great weekend in Greece with the VanderWeeles. Thassos was beautiful, and I would one day love to come back here on my honeymoon. The ruins at Philippi are incredible. I felt so close to Jesus, walking the steps that Paul walked.

I am getting a little frustrated with the apartment scene. Also have a job opportunity with Frank Muncie's school. The board re-votes tomorrow on my application, so we will see.

The Bible studies are starting up this week. I am beginning to feel like I am more and more at home in this country. I must rely on the Lord more and not be so independent. I pray for more opportunities to meet new kids from the American College. Lord, please prepare some heart at that campus.

Every day, I felt more and more comfortable. I begin to appreciate the beauty here. There are some fabulous parks that provide hours of trails to run on. I start to learn my way around and no longer fear getting lost. I am continually confronted with the fact that Young Life is needed here. Wyld Life, which is the middle school ministry of Young Life, is growing and it is becoming the "thing to do," praise God! The older group was much harder to make contact with. I had to figure out a way to get to know the older kids better. The Anglo-American school shares a campus with The American School where the high school students attend, so we are in close proximity with them. We actually share a campus on the former communist training grounds just outside of town, but the schools are run by two different organizations that have nothing to do with each other. I prayed that some relationships would begin to develop a little deeper now. Marta continued to be a blessing I my life. I hoped I wouldn't wear out my welcome at their house.

Oct. 18, 1994

It is the morning of the big board meeting. I am fasting today and focusing my prayers on my job situation. Lord, I pray that they will change their minds. The harvest is plentiful at that campus. I would like to help the Muncies at their school but feel my efforts are better focused at the International School.

I talked to my parents this morning. That was a special lift and encouragement. I wish that it was easier to tell them all about Bulgaria, but not enough time and words cannot express what is' happening here.

Some exciting things are happening here with the students. Thank You, Lord. Each day brings a new adventure and experience.

Oct. 20, 1994

Well, the board voted no again. I met with the board president and he tried to explain their fears. I just don't understand how nine educated people could be so paranoid. It's absurd to think that by hiring me it would jeopardize the entire school's visa situation. He also said that he could guarantee me that Young Life will be written about and slammed in the local paper.

My frustrations are very high. It would be so easy to jump ship and go to a different country or home. Satan is trying his best to push me away. I decided to turn down the Muncie school and have faith that the board will reconsider next meeting if no one more suitable for the job applies. I just feel in my heart that this is where I need to be.

Howe was encouraging to talk to because he reminded me how well the actual club is going. Praise God. I would rather have Satan attack me personally than the ministry or children.

I could not believe that I was actually losing my job because of my Christian faith. You hear about missionaries across the world being persecuted for their faith, but I was fired by fellow Americans. Thankfully, my parents were friends with Senator Tilman Bishop from Colorado. He made a few phone calls on my behalf to the ambassador to let him know that he was aware of what was going on. I am sure that the American ambassador was cursing the day he met Howe and me and the senators who represented us back home, because his abuse of power was being exposed.

The saying, "when one door closes, another door opens" is so true when God is in control. I was offered a teaching job at the American English Academy, and until things got worked out, I needed to take the job. Just when I was wondering if I was going to be able to afford to stay, God provided. I also spend time praying about leaving Bulgaria and moving on to another international school in a different country. There is an international school job fair in London that I could go to in order to find a job.

"Lord, is this Your will or is this me just running scared?"

Oct. 27, 1994

Working at the American English Academy has been a change of pace. It is nice teaching science again. The battle at the Anglo-American school continues. I am really considering going to the job fair in England in January. My prayer is that I would listen to the Lord and not Satan. Father, make Your will known to me. If it is for me to stay, so be it. If it is for me to go, please provide someone here to take my place.

I have really been longing for a boyfriend lately, and my ex-boyfriend has been in my thoughts often. Lord, thank You for providing an apartment. I pray that You would guide and bless the flat and us four living there.

From PE Teacher to Kidnapper!

Oct. 31, 1994

Well, tonight is my last night staying with Steve and Marta. They have been a huge answer to prayer, and I am really going to miss them. I am anxious about living with these other women, Lord. Please lay Your hand on our friendship. Help me to be the best roommate that I can be. One gal is a teacher to the Nazarene missionary kids and the other is a young Bulgarian Christian. I went back to the Anglo-American School today. Those kids are really great. They have started a petition to get me reinstated as a teacher there.

Nov. 3, 1994

I wrote my letter of interest for the teaching fair in London. Lord, please guide me. Let me know if I should leave Bulgaria and where I should go. I pray that my checkbook would show up soon.

Nov. 4, 1994

I finally moved into my apartment and am getting settled. It was hard leaving the Gillilans. They have been such a blessing. I think the honeymoon period has worn off and I am in the low part of transition. Lord, give me strength to endure. I have had so many doubts about being in Bulgaria for two years. The fear of the government and life keep me from holding firm to my two-year commitment.

The living situation is going to be very challenging and take the Lord's grace to bless and watch over it. We all live, act, and eat so differently. I am feeling like an outsider who got the worst room. Lord, help me not to have such self-pity. I should be very thankful for Christian sisters in Bulgaria.

Talking to Linda VanderWeele is always nice for me. I like spending time with that family. Thank You also for the Oosterhouses. They are a warm, encouraging family. What great hearts, and their kids are amazing.

Praise God that Marta is pregnant. Please, Lord, protect her child as it grows. May it grow to love and serve You.

One great thing about my new apartment was that it was closer to the school and had a soccer field alongside. So, most days after school, the middle school kids would gather here. We would kick the ball around, and they would come up for snacks. It proved to be such a blessing and a great chance to spend more time with these kids. Little did I know that what I thought to be a great opportunity to reach out to the kids was something that would backfire on me. One day, I arrived home and the police were there and arrested me. My neighbors had turned me in for kidnapping and selling kids to the United States. I was allowed make a phone call and get help, so I called the VanderWeeles, who hired a lawyer for me. I was allowed to go home, but I spent my days in the small room with a desk and three chairs—one for me, one for my lawyer, and one for the interrogator. The bizarre thing was that the line of interrogation was toward what my parents did, how they met, where they lived, and that sort of thing. The interrogator never really asked me anything about why the kids were hanging out at my house, which was good, because you did have to be careful about publicly declaring your faith in Christ. The interrogation took three days because the interrogator would ask the questions in Bulgarian, my lawyer would translate, and then I would answer. However, they would not let the lawyer speak for me, so my lawyer had to tell me how to say my response in Bulgarian. After three full days of enduring this line of questioning, I was cleared and released. There was no explanation for their suspicions and no apology for disrupting my life for three days. The day I was released, I had lunch with the American defense attaché and his family. They told me that their entire home is actually bugged so that the Bulgarian government can keep tabs on them. When I got home that night, I found several of my wall outlets had been removed. Lo and behold, the bugs that had been placed in my apartment had been removed!

Nov. 15, 1994

> *I had lunch with one of the school board members today. She says my not being hired is strictly for religious reasons. The evil forces are at work, but I KNOW that God has a plan and everything will work out one way or another. I have begun to feel a burden for this American*

girl, Alison. One parent is a Christian, the other Jewish, and unbeknownst to them, their grandparents are financially supporting my ministry.

It was time once again to take a trip to Greece for more food. This time, however, proved to be much more than we bargained for. The road from Sophia, Bulgaria, to Thessaloniki, Greece, is mountainous. It is a windy, two-lane road with a lot of semi trucks transporting goods. On this trip, there was a bad accident that had the road shut down for about five hours. The problem was that Marts was pregnant, which means she contained a pregnant woman's bladder. Being the conservative woman that she is, we concocted this plan that we would open the passenger side front and back doors and Marta squatted between them with the mountains on the side to give her total protection. The only thing we didn't account for was the downhill sloping road and the river she caused. Now, everyone downstream had to step out of the way, knowing exactly what she had done. We eventually made it into Greece, where we binged on McDonald's and shopped for another month's worth of food.

CHAPTER 3

Knocked Down, but Not Out

One thing I know for sure is that food speaks to a man's heart. So when I was in Greece over the weekend, I bought some ground beef and cheese to add to my taco seasoning and taco shells from the American commissary. To top off the meal, I had the *piece de resistance*: a cheesecake from Greece. I called up the five Nazarene boys and offered to cook them all dinner to show my appreciation for their help as volunteer leaders. The only problem was that I had to cook at their place, since my kitchen and apartment were too small. So I packed the food into two bags and hopped on the bus to their house. Sitting on the bus to their flat, as I clenched my bags tightly, my mind started to wander; I thought about what I was going to do when these guys returned to the United States and I didn't have their help. I was getting sad thinking about missing their friendship and not having guys to minister to these boys. They loved playing soccer with the middle school boys, and I could never replace them. A horn honked and snapped me out of my lament. I noticed that I had missed my bus stop, so I grabbed my bags and got off at the next stop. I knew that I was close, but was not exactly sure where I was, since I had never been to their place before. I saw a row of taxi drivers, and remembering the name of a popular restaurant that was directly across from their flat, I confidently asked a driver in my best Bulgarian if he knew were this restaurant was. He moved his head up and down and said, "ne." I had to think for a minute, because his head shake said yes, but his voice said no. In Bulgaria, moving your head from side to side means yes and up and down means no. I walked to the next cab and then to a third cab. Finally, I found a driver who spoke English! He said that he knew where I wanted to go and would take me there. So I climbed into the back seat with my bags in tote, and off we went.

About ten minutes into the ride, I realized that we were going in the wrong direction. We were actually driving away from town. I told him to turn around, but he drove on. I asked him to stop and let me out, but he would not. As we approached Ring Road—a road that circles the entire city—I knew I was in trouble. It was getting dark outside, and this man was not going to let me go. As we neared each intersection, he would slow down, look right then left, and then press on through the stop sign. As I looked back, I could see the lights of Alexander Nevski Cathedral getting farther and farther away. I knew I had to do something. So, after going through four stop signs, I decided that at the next stop sign, I would open the door and jump out—cheesecake and all! As we approached the stop sign and the taxi driver slowed down, I opened the door, grabbed my bags, and jumped out. I did sort of a fireman's roll and came to a stop. With so much adrenaline pumping through my body, it never occurred to me that I could actually hurt myself. I looked up, and luckily the taxi drove on. As I dusted off my pants, I picked up my groceries and began to walk toward the lights of Nevski Cathedral up on the hill, because I knew that if I could get there, I would know how to get home. Several times, police cars drove past me, but the police were not to be trusted. I had heard stories of how they had beaten and robbed other Americans. I was very thankful that my with my dark hair and dark overcoat, I looked Bulgarian. Four hours later, I arrived back at my house, where a search party was forming and prayers were being thrown up for my safety.

Nov. 23, 1994

Today was one of the hardest days of my life. I received my visa but was denied the job. Then I had a life-threatening event. I have never felt so helpless as tonight in the street. I was lost and could not communicate with anyone. I ended up on the wrong side of town and completely disoriented. I did not know who that man was or what he wanted, but I knew it wasn't good. The guys were waiting for dinner, and I was very scared. I couldn't go to the police for help, because they would probably take me too.

I am so glad that tomorrow is Thanksgiving and I will be at Steve and Marta's all day. Lord, I pray for guidance and discernment. My desire to leave here is growing and so is my guilt to stay here. I feel that all Americans are going to be forced out soon. This country is collapsing before me.

Nov. 24, 1994

It's Thanksgiving Day, and we are without water and electricity! Yet the sun is shining and I have so much to be thankful for. I have recovered from my traumatic experience last night. The weather is starting to turn, and my spirits are really fluctuating. I feel at times like I am really alone here. I pray for a friend that I can share activities, prayers, and dreams with.

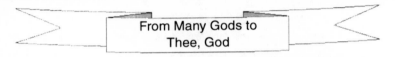

From Many Gods to Thee, God

I was both dreading and looking forward to the Christmas vacation. Everyone I knew was going home for the holidays, and I was staying here. I knew that if I went home, I would never return; God was not done with me here. Luckily, I was going to be house-sitting for the Gillilans, and they had a TV. They also had a nice Indian family who lived next door. The kids would come over and keep me company, and the mother brought over great Indian food. Christmas Eve, I went to the American Baptist church where Pastor Duke, his wife, and I were the only Americans. Everyone else was Nigerian. I had also been invited to Christmas Eve dinner with the Van Stackhausens, so after church, I enjoyed a great German-style Christmas. The night concluded with singing of "Stille Nacht"— *"Silent Night"* in German.

I awoke Christmas morning with such loneliness; my family and friends were halfway around the world. I know that God is with me and has given me the best gift this Christmas—eternal life—and this brings me comfort and the strength to persevere here.

Dec. 25, 1994 morning

Merry Christmas, Jesus! I spent more time in prayer today than I have in a long time. The day seemed almost like any other day. It was easier being alone today than last night at church. I reflected a lot about the people in my life that I love and care for. My appreciation for them has grown. I received a present from the Bowmans today and that was wonderful. They have played such an important role in my life and faith.

It was great talking to my family today. I pray that Nonna is happy and healthy. My attitude toward many things has changed since I've been here. I value people, friends, and relationships more than ever. Why did I value achievements so much before? I can't explain the feeling in my heart, but it is changed and it is strong.

Two Indian Hindu children came over today. They are asking so many questions about Jesus and heaven. I pray that they may accept your gift, Lord.

Dec. 25, 1994 evening

As I sit down to write in my journal, my heart is aching. I want to go home so badly. The loneliness of the holidays has hit me hard. I pray that once school begins again, this feeling will go away. I can see why once a person gets lonely, depression sets in. I have been reading about many people that have suffered much more than I am. Lord, help me!

I went to bed that night more thankful for the presence of God than I had ever been in my life. I was woken up the next day by knocking on the door. It was the Hindu boy Sandeep who lives next door. He and his sister had come over every day to borrow videos to pass the time. I told him that they had watched all the videos we had except one, *The Jesus Film*, by the Navigators. He said he wanted to watch it, and I suggested that he watch it with me instead of at his house. As Sandeep watched and learned about Jesus, he crept closer and closer to the TV set. At the conclusion of the video, when they asked the viewers to join them in the prayer of salvation, this precious young middle school boy—who dreamed of being the first Indian in space—gave his life to Jesus. This was the best Christmas present I could have ever asked for. Even more, I sent him home with a Bible to read, and the next day, he returned with his younger sister, who began relaying all these "crazy" stories her brother was telling her of a man who walked on water and healed the sick and blind. He had read all four gospels in one night! And he relayed the stories to her with such enthusiasm, yet she thought he was trying to pull her leg. I assured her that they were true accounts and that Jesus did everything Sandeep claimed he did. That afternoon, his mother knocked on the door with a plate of hot samosas and said to me, "It doesn't matter what religion people are, but what matters is that they never change their religion." It won't be long until she sees a difference in Sandeep and knows God has changed him.

For the first time in my life, Christmas was about the birth and gift of our Savior, not about Angie Feather. God was teaching me so much. Thank You, God, for rocking my world and ruffling my feathers and showing me that You are victorious. The words of David in Psalm 139 pierced my heart and it was at this point that I memorized this psalm and it began to heal my soul.

O LORD, you have searched me and you know me.
[2] You know when I sit and when I rise; you perceive my thoughts from afar.
[3] You discern my going out and my lying down; you are familiar with all my ways.
[4] Before a word is on my tongue you know it completely, O LORD.
[5] You hem me in—behind and before; you have laid your hand upon me.
[6] Such knowledge is too wonderful for me, too lofty for me to attain.
[7] Where can I go from your Spirit? Where can I flee from your presence?

⁸ If I go up to the heavens, you are there; if I make my
bed in the depths, [a] you are there.
⁹ If I rise on the wings of the dawn, if I settle on the far
side of the sea,
¹⁰ even there your hand will guide me, your right hand
will hold me fast.
¹¹ If I say, "Surely the darkness will hide me and the
light become night around me,"
¹² even the darkness will not be dark to you; the night
will shine like the day, for darkness is as light to you.
¹³ For you created my inmost being; you knit me
together in my mother's womb.
¹⁴ I praise you because I am fearfully and wonderfully
made; your works are wonderful,
I know that full well.
¹⁵ My frame was not hidden from you when I was made
in the secret place.
When I was woven together in the depths of the earth,
¹⁶ your eyes saw my unformed body.
All the days ordained for me were written in your book
before one of them came to be.
¹⁷ How precious to [b] me are your thoughts, O God!
How vast is the sum of them!
¹⁸ Were I to count them, they would outnumber the
grains of sand.
When I awake,
I am still with you.
¹⁹ If only you would slay the wicked, O God!
Away from me, you bloodthirsty men!
²⁰ They speak of you with evil intent; your adversaries
misuse your name.
²¹ Do I not hate those who hate you, O LORD, and
abhor those who rise up against you?

> [22] *I have nothing but hatred for them;*
> *I count them my enemies.*
> [23] *Search me, O God, and know my heart; test me and*
> *know my anxious thoughts.*
> [24] *See if there is any offensive way in me, and lead me*
> *in the way everlasting.*

New Year's Eve was another lonely point. I was warned not to go outside because everyone shoots off guns, and the falling bullets have been known to kill people. So I stayed inside and spent the night with the band Arrested Development as they performed live on MTV, and I felt very sorry for myself.

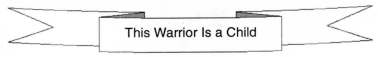

This Warrior Is a Child

The frustration over where I would live continued. Things did not work out with the two other missionary women I moved in with, so now I lived with the Gillilans. Wyld Life, the middle school group, was growing stronger. I told them about the cross and that Jesus died for their sins, and they really listened. I prayed for Samantha (American), Juliana (German), Sasha (Bulgarian), and Don (Indian). God, I will boldly preach Your Word here, yet I feel it's more about what You do *in* me rather than *through* me right now. I am beginning to get homesick. The newness and excitement of living in Bulgaria has worn off. The adventure that was finding food and water and avoiding rabid dogs was once thrilling, but it has grown stale. I am really ready to move into my own apartment. I need to get on a regular eating, sleeping, praying, studying, and meditating schedule. I pray that this will happen soon. I coached the middle school girls' basketball team, and we just got back from a weekend tournament in Bucharest, Romania. The girls played great and enjoyed themselves. Bucharest is about five to eight years ahead of Sofia in my eyes. They even have a KFC!

I can't express my feelings, but I want to leave Bulgaria badly. I grow more and more depressed, and I haven't ever felt this way before. I am forced to lean on and look to God more and more. I am definitely in one of those serious molding stages of life. My contract with the school ends next Friday and my Young Life financial support has been cut to a third. My near future is so cloudy, yet I have a calmness and peace because I trust in God. I know that He is truly in control. He has proven to me lately no matter what has happened, is happening, or will happen, He is with me and is using all things for good. I know that whenever I look back on this time of my life, I will smile and thank God. But for now, this independent, strong, and proud woman feels like a child. I listened to Twila Paris over and over as I fill up the bottle of tears God has stored for me.

Lately I've been winning battles left and right
But even winners can get wounded in the fight
People say that I'm amazing
Strong beyond my years
But they don't see inside of me
I'm hiding all the tears

They don't know that I go running home when I fall down
They don't know who picks me up when no one is around
I drop my sword and cry for just a while
'Cause deep inside this armor
The warrior is a child

Unafraid because His armor is the best
But even soldiers need a quiet place to rest
People say that I'm amazing
Never face retreat
But they don't see the enemies
That lay me at His feet

They don't know that I go running home when I fall down
They don't know who picks me up when no one is around
I drop my sword and cry for just a while
'cause deep inside this armor
the warrior is a child

They don't know that I go running home when I fall down
They don't know who picks me up when no one is around
I drop my sword and look up for a smile
'cause deep inside this armor
Deep inside this armor
Deep inside this armor
The warrior is a child

Can You Say *Lawsuit*?

To add insult to injury, other unexpected problems popped up. One day, I took the eighth-grade class to a local gym to put on a basketball clinic with them. During the practice, a ball was thrown away and one of my more aggressive basketball girls, Alison, ran after it. There was a curtain separating the basketball court from the volleyball court, so I could not see what happened. The next thing I hear is this blood-curdling scream from Alison, so I ran around the curtain toward her. I saw her lying on the ground, holding her leg. I assumed she tripped and sprained her ankle. But as I got closer to her, I could see that her pants were ripped on the upper right thigh. I grabbed her hand and tried to calm her down while I peeked at her leg through the hole in her jeans. When I pulled back the jean material just slightly, I could see femur bone. She had sliced through her leg to the bone.

Now I had a problem! I was the only adult in this gym, because we had been dropped off by the school bus, and it would not return for another hour. There were no phones to call for help, to call the school, or to call her parents. I was so thankful for the summer I spent volunteering at the hospital, so I was somewhat comfortable with open wounds. Thank God at this point it was not bleeding. I would not let Alison look at her leg, because I knew she would go into shock. No missionary or educational training could prepare you for such a scenario. I had to do something quickly, so I sent two kids to find the man who ran the gym. He flagged down two taxi cabs for me. I picked the three most responsible eighth graders (if there is such a thing) and sent them back to the school in one cab so they could let them know what happened. I took Alison and a Bulgarian girl, Milana, with me to translate, and we headed to the local hospital. The rest of the kids were to wait at the gym for the school to pick them up. Does this scream *lawsuit* here in the United States or what?

When we got to the hospital, I did a quick assessment to see if things were sterile, and it looked good to me. They took Alison into a room and would not let me go with her. I stood outside the door with it cracked open so I could see what was going on. They did allow Milana in there to translate, since Alison, an American, did not speak Bulgarian. The problem was that Milana had a very weak stomach. The moment they cut away the jeans material, the wound started gushing blood. The next thing I heard was a thump—Milana fainted and was on the ground. It was at this point that I demanded to be in the room to supervise what was going on. I was very impressed with the doctor who stitched her up from the inside out.

Just as the doctors finished up, Alison's parents and the embassy doctor came running into the hospital. Instead of being thankful for saving their daughter's life, they threatened a lawsuit because I had not received their permission or called the embassy doctor because, after all, she is the daughter of two diplomats. It was clear to me now why God had placed them on my heart over the past month to pray for them. Needless to say, the embassy doctor evaluated the wound and concluded that they did a fine job of stitching her up. And all the kids made it back to the school safe and sound.

Jan. 26, 1995

*The Lord is so faithful. Here I sit one week after I was
ready to give up, and I feel great. God provided a job,
an apartment, and a renewed energy and enthusiasm for
sharing the gospel. And the sun is shining. Praise God.*

*What a day yesterday was. I spent the entire morning
at the hospital with Alison. It was so frustrating. I felt
once again completely helpless. There was no phone and
no way to get help. God forced me to turn to Him. I am
so thankful for my experience at St. Mary's. It was quite
funny when Milana fainted at the sight of Alison's leg.*

*I signed my new contract for the rest of the year.
Plus they asked me to teach an ethics and morals class.
God works in such mighty ways. I wonder what God's
plan for Alison is. I sure have had a chance to have a lot
of contact with her. Lord, keep using me to accomplish
Your purpose.*

Feb. 21, 1995

*Happy birthday to me! Today I turn twenty-four
years old. My day was spent on the ski slopes. It was a
beautiful day and the snow is melting. I remember last
year on this day coaching basketball, running the hills
in Colorado, and going to Dos Hombres for dinner with
my family. It is amazing how much things can change
in one year's time. It seems like only yesterday that life
was so easy. As I turn one year older, I feel wiser, more
youthful, and old all at the same time. At times, I long
to be married, and at times, I cherish my singleness. I*

do miss dating and the excitement of a special friend. Overall it was a year of ups and downs. I was at my spiritual low, but now have come so far. Thank You, Lord. And thank You for the wonderful, God-loving parents that You gave to me.

Feb. 28, 1995

I am finally moved and settled into my own place. It is very nice, but a little lonely. I have been spending more time with the Lord. Acts 20:24 has really become inspiring to me. "However, I consider my life worth nothing to me, if only I may finish the race and complete the task the Lord Jesus has given me-the task of testifying to the gospel of God's grace." Our Thursday night Bible study is going to be good. Club numbers were down this week. I must continue to let the Lord use me and let my light shine before me.

I have been longing for a close friend the last couple of days. Once again, I find myself thinking about past dating relationships and questioning if any of them were God's best for me as a husband. I have been dreaming about my future family a lot lately, probably because many of my friends here are married with babies or pregnant. Lard, I pray for my future husband and family.

Rob (one of the Nazarenes) was poisoned by an old man who bought him a cup of coffee. His watch and wallet were stolen. He woke up in the basement of a warehouse. Lord, please heal him quickly and protect him.

We had water that day, so I got up early and did some laundry. Since there were no clothes dryers, I had to hang everything on my balcony. I also had my first bout with food poisoning, to the point that nothing will stay in me. I went to the kiosk down the street to get a Sprite to help settle my stomach. When I returned, all of my clothes had blown off the line and were up higher into the tree in the courtyard. I had to go upstairs to my neighbor's door and with motions and gestures explain what I needed so I could go out on his balcony with a stick and try to retrieve some of my clothes. Add that to my sickness, and my spirits were down. I wrote a song with the guitar to express myself. It's no Twila Paris, but it expressed my heart.

> *You have called me, You have called me*
> *To be a rock in a hard place.*
> *I am searching, I am looking*
> *But my eyes are failing me.*

> *Where have You gone?*
> *Where have You gone?*
> *My foes surround me, they cretanize me*
> *Where can I find the strength to carry me?*

> *We walk, yes, we walk,*
> *We walk, yes, we walk,*
> *We walk in the power of God.*
> *We walk, yes, we walk*
> *We walk in the power of God every day.*

> *You have saved me, You have saved me*
> *Not by my works but by Your grace.*
> *I must finish the race I'm running,*
> *And complete the task You've given to me.*

I am thankful, I am thankful
For without trials, where would I be?
You have called me, You are with me,
You have saved me by Your loving grace.

Thankfully, tomorrow night is our weekly basketball game where the american missionaries take on the american diplomats at Sofia University. This always brightened up my spirits, even if I was the only female playing. We missionaries had some great athletes as Campus Crusade for Christ has a strong presence there and we always won. This seems to be the only time during my week that I can relax and let my guard down and just enjoy a healthy distraction. With all that is happening to and around me and in the lives of kids, a respite is needed once in a while to refresh the body and soul. For if it wasn't for such moments in my life to recuperate, I might just hop on a plane and flee to greener, safer pastures.

CHAPTER 4

Spring Break in the Holy Land

The attacks never seemed to stop. Thankfully, the Lord sent His protective angels to watch over me once again. I was on my way to get water from a well in the woods, and a man started following me. He followed me for a while and then began to yell and make sexual gestures. He unzipped his pants and then chased me. I ran across a field and down a hill, then across a highway and up the other side, where there were many people. That was the most afraid I had been in a long time. I knew that there were many faithful people, including my parents, praying for my protection back home, and I believed that there was a direct connection between the prayers of these faithful people and my continued safety. Then, not five minutes later, I saw a group of twenty high school students guzzling beer. What a sinful world we live in.

Mar. 29, 1995

> *Food poisoning again! What an awful thing. I've been in bed for almost forty-eight hours now. Hot and cold, headaches, absolutely nothing will stay in me. I need my mom! If I do drink some water, I cramp up right away. Plus there is a major blizzard outside. I am tired of the snow and I am tired of Bulgaria.*

Tonight I am supposed to be going to the Bulgaria vs. Whales soccer game, but I know I won't have the strength.

After three days of vomiting, I was finally able to hold down some liquids. Thank God that it was over—food poisoning once again. One thing that I came to realize about international school kids is that they have experienced a lot in their life and you can't really "wow" them with stuff. Back in the United States, the Young Life camps are so spectacular that it is the best place some kids have ever been. These kids, on the other hand, have been to the pyramids in Egypt, climbed the Great Wall, and any and everything else you can think of. So I decided that doing volunteer work at an orphanage might have that "wow" factor for them.

I don't know how to describe what we saw when we arrived at this orphanage just outside of Sofia, but it took my breath away. It was a bitter cold day, and there was no heat in this building. The kids had light jackets, and only a few had shoes. The smell was enough to make you want to throw up and there were so many babies in one crib that they were lying on top of each other. I think we were all scared at first, but after a while, the middle school kids slowly began to play with the orphans. The boys played soccer and the girls picked up and held the babies. It was the most precious sight I had ever seen. We brought the orphans a soccer ball, some clothes, and a few other toys. But what we took home from that day was priceless.

Apr. 1, 1995

What an experience it is to take a group of middle school kids to a Bulgarian orphanage for the day. It is a win/win situation. The orphans love having other kids to play with them. The smiles on their faces could brighten

*the sky. The change or growth that occurs in our kids
is something as well. Your heart breaks for them. Lord,
please send someone to those children as an ambassador
for You. Lord, thank You for allowing me to experience
You today.*

*There is still a foot of snow on the ground, and I am
sick of it. We leave for Israel in a little over a week. I am
so looking forward to that.*

Today I received many letters from the great people at the Young
Life service center. It really ministered to me and said to wait on
the Lord for my next placement. The Lord has been so faithful to
me. What a fool I was to think that God doesn't have the next year
planned for me. When I am ready, God will let me know where He
wants me.

Sunrise Service at the Tomb

Today—April 14, 1995—I sit at the Sea of Galilee. There is no way
to explain in words what it is like. There is a cool breeze that comes
off the Golan Heights, and the smell of fresh fish is in the air. As I
breathe it all in, I can picture Jesus calming the storm and walking
on the water. It is smaller than I had imagined, but as the sun shines
down on my face, I can picture Jesus here. I can *feel* Jesus here. As
a tour group pulls in, I overhear the tour guide explaining that even
though the water is calm now, such a storm as the one described
where Jesus had to calm the wind and the waves is possible. I learned
how the storm is formed that would cause such an incredible storm.
It's the Arabian desert winds meeting the cooler winds off the Golan
Heights. When these two air masses collide, it cause a fierce storm
over the Sea of Galilee. It is almost too much for me to comprehend

all at once. There are so many Christian pilgrims who have come for Holy Week. They've come from all over the world. Your word, Jesus, has spread so far, yet there are so many more to reach. We went to Capernaum, Mount of Beatitudes, where Jesus multiplied two loaves of bread and one fish in order to feed the multitudes.

I traveled here with five other Americans from Bulgaria—a couple, Jon and Ann (who taught at my school) and their newborn baby boy, and Sam, the new PE teacher at my school, and one of the Nazarene missionaries named Todd. We all got along well, so we rented a fifteen-passenger van to drive throughout the country in. Ironically, the new PE teacher they hired is old drinking buddies with our headmaster! The great thing is that since our headmaster last saw Sam, he has become a Christian. God is so good and is full of pleasant surprises.

Apr. 14, 1995

> *I have just received word that there is a position open in Puerto Vallarta, Mexico, and they are trying to contact me. Lord, the situation is very unclear to me but not to You. Father, I pray that I would listen to You and not my desires. Lord, how will I know Your will? I could think of no better place to listen to You than Your homeland!*

> *Father, help me to keep in communion with You, because I am getting so caught up in the history that I'm not spending time meditating on You.*

> *Father, give me wisdom and peace as I listen for Your direction.*

Traveling throughout the Holy Land is as incredible as it is dangerous. We started our trip in a kibbutz our first night and then headed up to Haifa, where I discovered falafels. They became my lunch every day. I had to have a falafel. They sell these falafels like we sell hot dogs. There is a cart on the side of the where you buy the basic falafel, and then there are about twenty different condiments you can put in it. I have yet to find a falafel in the United States that compares to these. We went to the Sea of Galilee and the Jordan River, where Jesus was baptized. Then, after a few days of touring around there, we drove to Jerusalem for Good Friday and Easter. We joined thousands of other pilgrims walking the Stations of the Cross or Via Delarosa on Good Friday. I don't think that day will ever be the same for me again.

On Saturday, we drove down to the Dead Sea, which is so salty that you actually float. We even tried to load large rocks onto our stomachs in order to sink, but we did not. Then we hiked up to the ruins of Masada, where many years ago, thousands of Jewish rebels chose to kill themselves rather than be taken by the Romans. We then went on to the caves where the Dead Sea Scrolls were found and then on to Mt. Tabor (or the Mount of Transformation). I didn't realize how small Israel actually was. The distance from Jericho to Nazareth isn't really that great.

Old Jerusalem has to be the most fascinating place in the world. It is where four major religions meet and share walls. The four quarters where the Jewish, Armenian, Muslim, and Christian split this one square kilometer is surrounded by walls on all sides. Each quarter has its unique smells, foods, and merchandise unique to that culture. All of a sudden, you turn a corner and it's like you have entered a new world. One of the highlights for me was to go to the Wailing Wall. The tradition is to go there, write your prayer on a small piece of paper, and then find a crack in the wall so you can tuck your prayer into it. You are then literally giving it up to God. I asked God to heal Justin that day, so I put a prayer paper in the wall on his behalf.

Apr. 16, 1995

I never realized why it truly is called the Holy Land. I am still feeling a bit overwhelmed being here. I think that Galilee is my favorite spot. I can see why Jesus chose it as His hometown area. I wish that my family could be here to experience it all.

I feel like much more of a student of the Bible now. Lord, it is so commercialized and intense here that I have not found a quiet place to be alone with You. I am so sorry. Here I sit above Golgotha on Saturday night while You lay buried in the tomb fifty meters away. Tomorrow, You will rise and the whole world will believe that You are the Son of God. Yet if it were only I who was saved and believed You would have died. Lord, I in turn, owe You my life.

They Are Stoning Up Ahead

Imagine being at Jesus' tomb for the Easter sunrise service. We got up early and joined hundreds of others as we surrounded the cave where it is believed Jesus was buried and rose. Words cannot express the grief and gratitude that permeated my soul at that moment. There were no Easter bunnies or colored eggs and chocolate—just the risen Lord. Amazing!

We decided to make the most of the day and drive south to Beersheba, but the trip didn't go as expected. We loaded up the van and started on our way. When we got into a town called Hebron, we came to a checkpoint. Now, this is common practice in the area, but as tourists, we were always waved through without any problem. This time, it was different. The Israeli military at this stop informed us that if we went any further along this road, we would find Islamic militants were throwing stones up ahead in anger for two Shiite Muslims who were killed earlier that morning. Being a bit naïve to the severity of the situation, Jon, our driver, shrugged his shoulders and started to pull forward. Once again, the soldiers ran in front of our van and told us we must, for our own safety, turn around. Only when Jon was threatened by his wife that if he didn't turn around she would take his baby son and get out and walk did he turn around. Just as we started back down the hill we had just driven up, another group of soldiers ran in front of us to stop the van. They were yelling, but we couldn't understand what was going on.

They finally found a soldier who could speak English, and he informed us that there was a land mine in the middle of the road just ahead. This couldn't be the stretch of road we had just driven over about five minutes before! Soldiers and tanks were everywhere. As we looked around, we realized that there was no one else on the road and no pedestrians walking about. Unbeknownst to us, there was a curfew out because of the fear of retaliation for the death of those two men. So, here we sat between a rock and a bomb. Over the next three hours, we watched and filmed the bomb squad assemble and send a remote-control robot out to detonate the bomb. We knew that CNN would want this footage, so we kept filming; again, a bit too naïve to realize the life-threatening situation we were in. After it blew up, we were able to drive back the way we had come. Needless to say, we decided to head to the Tel Aviv airport and get out of there!

I tried calling the school in Puerto Vallarta one last time before boarding the plane. They must have been on spring break because no one answered the phone. I felt rather rushed, but I know that the Lord will guide me and my phone calls.

Apr. 25, 1995

> *My spirit is heavy today. I'm not sure why, but I am very homesick. I began a five-day fast to try and not give in to my temptations. Lord, I give You my life. Please help me not to worry about what I will eat or drink or about tomorrow, for You will provide.*

> *The school in Puerto Vallarta has offered me a PE position for next year. Plus they really want Young Life, as they have had a string of suicides with the international students. I pray, Lord, that You will guide me in a clear path one way or another. Right now, I cannot hear Your guiding words. Patience, Feather!*

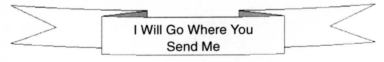

I Will Go Where You
Send Me

I decided to go to the job fair in London. At 8:43 AM, I was sitting at Gatwick Airport in London. The recruiting fair was small, and I was a bit disappointed in the number of schools there. However, there were a couple of new possibilities. The more I thought about Zurich, Switzerland, the more excited I became. I thought the potential for Young Life to thrive would be very high. I called Young Life's service center, and they informed me that there are several international churches there and that Young Life used to have a presence in the area. I came to realize over the year that I need help in ministry and can't do it alone any longer. I need to make sure that wherever I went, I would find a church and support group there. I would love to have a partner in ministry, so I asked Young Life if they could send someone to help me. I don't know if that's because I am lonely, feel inadequate, or really need the help. It seems biblical to me that you should minister in pairs. I hope that this new excitement is founded in the Lord's desires and not solely mine. The thought of being alone scares me and feel that if I stay overseas, I am putting my heart on hold again. I would also have to learn German, and I am just getting a grasp of Bulgarian.

May 7, 1995

> *I wonder if I should be in Mexico, Colombia, or Switzerland? Lord, may I hear Your word and Your will for my life.*

My decision to leave Bulgaria was not as hard as expected. This poor country seemed to be crumbling underneath us. Enrollment at the Anglo-American School has greatly decreased, and they will be putting the lower school (kindergarten to fourth grade) and upper school (fifth through eighth grades) on one campus. They also gave the teachers the option to get out of our contract because they needed to cut positions. I did not want to break my commitment, but circumstances beyond my control provided an out for me. I decided to take the job in Switzerland. I was nervous about many things, but I knew that God would provide. I prayed for one good friend there, someone who could be as much as Marta has been to me here. It's so wonderful how God works. I kept on believing that He had something amazing planned for me—and He did. He's more amazing than I could imagine.

Yet amid all of the celebrating, my world was shattered. My left heel had been hurting for months, so I decided to have it X-rayed. In

Sofia, there was one hospital where all they did was X-rays. I will never forget walking into this room about the size of a basketball gym and seeing approximately forty different X-ray machines. The sad and scary thing was that the X-ray technician stood next to you without even wearing a lead cover as you got zapped. There was a naked woman who had her breast scanned, a young boy who was crying hysterically who had his arm scanned, and an elderly woman, who had her leg scanned. The room was filled with many more hurt people. Each of us got X-rayed in the same room exposed to all the rays. Upon X-ray, I found two bone spurs. The doctor says that my running career is over. I have a very hard time accepting, believing, and dealing with this news. My physical fitness has been such an important part of my life. Surely, God wouldn't take that away from me, would He? I must get a second opinion. This last month and a half in Bulgaria is going to be very hard if I can't run.

May 16, 1995

So often, I question my own heart and motives. Is my decision to go to Switzerland selfish? Lord, I am very anxious about the move. Will I be as lonely there as I have been here? Will that loneliness result in an eating disorder like it has here? Lord, my prayer is that my food would be to do Your will.

May 19, 1995

Lately, God has really been teaching about becoming a woman of excellence. I am continually struck with a desire for the gift of discernment on how to act and when to speak. This probably means being a listener first—which is hard for me to do.

I decided to spend a month at the International School in Salzburg, Austria, to work summer school. It looks absolutely beautiful there, and it's where my favorite film, *The Sound of Music*, was shot. Mozart was born there and Hitler's Eagles Nest is close. I am so excited about this opportunity. They have also expressed an interest in Young Life.

A group from the school has decided to spend our final three-day weekend of the school year in Greece, sailing. I think I will go with them, but instead of sailing, I will find a place to have my own personal retreat. I need time to process all that has happened to me and in me during my year here in Bulgaria.

May 28, 1995

Today is Justin's birthday. I miss him very much as well as the rest of my family. Here I sit on the beach in Port Cas, Greece. The weather is beautiful, and the scenery is incredible. As I read and pray, one thing keeps coming to mind: put yourself behind and take up your cross and follow Me! Nothing else matters!

Once again, I have changed my plans and will be heading home on June 18. I am feeling quite lonely again. My desires to meet a man continue to grow stronger. Lord, may I meet a man who will bring my gifts out of me and vice versa, not squash them.

My anxieties about Zurich have subsided a little, as God has shown me just to be myself. Lord, give me strength and discernment on overcoming my fears of stepping on people's toes or scaring them away from the gospel. May my love for You supersede my anxieties.

The last day of school was very emotional, as so many kids were moving on. One young girl wrote and composed a song for me to thank me for all I did for her. She recorded it and played it for me after class. Lord, please love, strengthen, and comfort her. It is hard to leave many of these kids here, but I know that they are in Your hands, God. As this chapter of my life closes, I both rejoice and am saddened. I have grown immensely, but my strength to live here has been sapped. I have been blessed to have spent a year with so many of these wonderful young people. I am so thankful for the Gillilans and all they did for me. Lord, when I take my eyes off myself and look to You, I see more of the picture and realize why I wasn't given the PE job.

I can't believe that my year here has come to an end. At 5:00 PM tomorrow, I will leave what has been one of the hardest years of my life. People are trying to prepare me for the culture shock of going back to the United States. I am very anxious and nervous about the summer and being back home; I am not the same person I was when I left. Yet even today, confirmation comes that it is time to leave. Walking home from the bus stop with one arm clenching my purse and the other holding up my umbrella, a man walking by thought he would cop a free feel and grabbed my breast. The assaults just keep on coming.

Jun. 18, 1995

Thank You, Lord, for this year, and may I use it to become a women of excellence. Here I met the God of the universe—not just the Young Life God. I value relationships more than ever before. I rediscovered who Angie Feather is without any type of label. I learned enormous patience and to accept many things as they

are. Christmas Day made me realize that God just wants
me to be available to Him.

This has been the single hardest year of my life, but I would not change it for anything. God showed me part of who He created me to be, by tearing away those manmade labels that I wore all of these years. Can I say I love the Lord with all my strength, heart, and mind? I can say I obey Him. I can serve Him. I can worship Him, but can I love Him with all that I am? God, I want so much to love You will all of my heart, mind, and soul. May I learn to transcend with my mind into my heart and stand there before You, in the love of God.

God, I don't want to put my heart on hold any longer. I want Your love to fill me up. I don't want to keep putting more and more protective layers around it or to act as if I don't long to be loved. Lord, I want to long to be loved by You!

CHAPTER 5

I Feel Like Heidi

Do you know that feeling when God takes you from the desert to the mountaintop? I have literally come to the mountaintop, the top of Zug, Switzerland. The International School of Zug was very thoughtful and found an apartment for me before I arrived. They asked if I preferred to live in the city or outside the city where I could run and bike. I chose to be outside of the city—but little did I know what they had chosen for me.

I was picked up from the airport by a fellow teacher, and he took me to my new place. We began to drive away from Zurich along Lake Zurich and then headed up the Zugerburg (or "Mt. Zug"). We then turned into this driveway that wound its way around a cattle barn and then a sheep barn, then over a creek to a beautiful house. Boy, was this place remote but beautiful. We knocked on the door, and this horse of a man answered and showed me to my place. They sure do grow these Swiss men big! We walked up the extremely steep spiral staircase to the attic. The apartment was made of wood with a roof that sloped from seven feet on one end to three on the other. My family room window faced the front of the house with a perfect view of the Swiss Alps, accompanied by the clanging of cow bells and the bleating of sheep. It was picturesque and I felt like Heidi—such a far cry from Bulgaria. My spirit was at peace, and I had all the trails I ever needed to run and bike on—and the hills truly were alive with the sound of music.

Then, one night, as I was coming home late, I was surrounded by a thick fog. As I pulled off Zugerstrasse onto my driveway, I slammed on the brakes. I saw that one of the sheep from this farm had gotten out of its pen and was in the middle of the road. I didn't know what to do, so I decided to wake up the farmer and his wife to let them know. As I approached their front door, I could hear him snoring. I began to knock on the door, but after a few minutes, it was clear he could not hear me over the snoring, so I started to pound on the door. This was not working, and the sheep was still loose, so I decided to go knock on the door of the farmhand who lived in a room under my staircase. I knocked and knocked on his door, and finally, I heard some grunting from inside. When he came to the door, he opened it just a crack, just enough so I could see all the way down his left side—and to my surprise, he was naked. Now I was faced with a dilemma. I had to keep eye contact with him because I didn't want to see anything else, but I also had to tell him a sheep was out of the pen. The only problem was that I didn't know enough German to explain the situation clearly. So I did the next best thing and started acting like a sheep and baa-ing to him, as I, again, tried to keep my eyes focused on his. Finally he raised his finger like he had an idea, closed the door, and then returned with a dictionary—a German-Portuguese dictionary. He didn't speak German either. So I motioned for a piece of paper so I could draw a picture to explain the problem. He opened the door so I could come in and draw on his entry table. So, there I was drawing a picture of a sheep jumping over the fence onto the street, all the while standing next to a naked Portuguese man. Finally between the drawing, baa-ing, and gesturing, he figured it out! He put some pants on, grabbed his umbrella, and went outside. Meanwhile, I walked up the stairs to my apartment, amazed at what just transpired. Needless to say, two nights later when another sheep got out of the pen—I left it alone!

Sept. 11, 1995

I've been in Zurich a month now and am having my first quiet evening home. I've never worked so hard at school or put in so many hours. I hope things settle down a bit. The running is super here. I can't say enough about the scenery. It's gorgeous. I've met a lot of nice folks; no Christian friends yet but God has blessed my few weeks here.

Most kids here have a lot of money, a lot of freedom, and very little guidance. I feel like this is a very tough group to minister to, but then again, that's why I am here. I am excited about the ministry here but still very anxious about finding leaders and starting a club. O ye of little faith!

The prices of things are unbelievable here. It cost $10 for a Happy Meal at McDonald's. Pizza Hut just opened up, and I had this brilliant idea to take a few key students and treat them to pizza. I just about choked on my soda when the bill arrived and each pizza was $100. I asked the kids if they could pitch in and buy their drinks. Gulp! I've gone from one of the poorest countries in the world to perhaps the richest country.

I need to get involved with a support group. I found a church in Zurich about thirty minutes away. I also need to spend more time in prayer. Why do I always start things off by trying to do it by myself?? So many prayers of loneliness have been answered. God is so good. Father, may I strive to give every moment to You. Lord, see if there is any offensive way in me and lead me in the way everlasting.

From the Desert to the Swiss Mountaintop

My first order of business was to establish a committee. One lesson I really learned in Bulgaria is that there is no Lone Ranger in ministry. Jesus' disciples all went out in two or more, and I needed to build a team if this ministry was to be healthy and sustainable. I found a fabulous church called International Protestant Church (IPC) of Zurich with Pastor Scott Herr at the helm. I set up a meeting with Pastor Scott to share the vision of Young Life and our need to partner with the church. It sounded like the International School of Zurich will be very open to Young Life as well. The next step would be forming the committee and leadership team. Many ideas raced through my head. Father, may I only try and run as fast as Your guiding light directs. I was introduced to Fred and Susan Harberg and to a single guy named Jeff Varick. Our friendships grew quickly, and they became fast friends and my support group. The Harbergs headed up the committee, and Jeff became my key volunteer. The Harbergs are a family with three kids; they all loved the Lord and loved serving Him—and they aren't even missionaries! God was blessing me in so many ways.

I spent most of my weekends walking or running around the beautiful lakes. I had a nice time as I walked alone with the Lord.

Sept. 17, 1995

> *I need to spend more time with the Lord. Whatever happened to giving every moment to Him and in communion with Him at all times? I am really feeling at home here and find it a lovely place to work and live. My prayer is that this is God's restoration, recuperation, and plan for me and not Satan distracting me from my*

goal. When things are going well, I tend to forget the Lord. Lord, forgive me for that and thank You for the many blessing that You have given me this year.

The committee grew steadily as a few more volunteer leaders jumped on board, and I even became a part of the singles group at IPC. My strength was returning, and my spirit was being refreshed. I didn't realize the depths of depression I had fallen into until I got here and came out of the fog and landed on the mountaintop. Even though it was at a middle school, teaching was going great, and the ministry was growing. Yet again, I began to struggle with food and body image. I find myself in this vicious cycle of starving myself, eating a ton, and then trying to run it off, only to feel worse and worse. God, I need You to be the food that sustains me!

Sept. 25, 1995

How often do I dwell on the past? I am so caught up with things that I've done right or wrong that I am not looking to what I will do. My selfishness is continually brought out. Lord, take it away. I must stand firm against temptation because You have given me all I need to resist it. Discipline!

E-mail has been a wonderful blessing in my life. I can't believe that I can write to people and send a message through the computer. Thank You, God, for allowing me to connect with friends back home this way. This alone helps stave off loneliness. Father, I thank You and praise You for my living conditions here and abundance of friends. You deserve all the praise.

In mid-October, I went to Munich, Germany, to meet up with the other European International School area directors and Youth for Christ staff. It was very encouraging. We began to plan a two-week-long service project to build a school at an orphanage in Romania. I returned home from that weekend encouraged and on fire for the Lord. The Lord then began to work among the international community in Zurich. I called eight couples about being on the committee, and seven agreed to go to an informational meeting. The hardest part about being an area director for me is working with the adults and asking for help. I had a vision, but I couldn't express it very well, but they caught the enthusiasm and passion I had for the teenagers and worked with me. I also built some great friendships with students at both Zug International School and the International School of Zurich. The International Church of Zurich, the International Baptist Church, and the Anglican church of Zurich have all came together with a common vision to reach the international kids in the Zurich area. This really felt like a team and that God was working in the hearts of young people. Many of these kids were expected to become ambassadors or presidents of large companies when they grow older. Imagine how much influence they would have as believers were they to accept Jesus into their hearts. The pressures are great for them, and their need for a savior is even greater. Now that we had developed some relationships, we decided to start club after Christmas.

Overall, I loved living and working in Switzerland. I also decided to leave this fabulous cottage on the mountaintop for civilization. I found a great three-bedroom condo right on Lake Zurich and an intern from the International Protestant Church to live with me. I was excited about having a roommate again. I missed the cows, but it would be good for my social life.

God has such a good sense of humor. On my last morning living in the cottage, as I was driving down my long driveway, I heard an awful noise coming from the barn. The farmer must have heard my car driving past, because he ran out and motioned for me to follow him. Since he was rather large and kind of scared me, I did what he said. Little did I know that a cow was giving birth and he needed my help. Of course, this could only happen to me. Where is the naked Portuguese man when you need him? Needless to say, I was a little late for school that day and had some blood on my shirt—but I had delivered a calf!

Living in civilization also has its disadvantages, as my new apartment proved. Their Swiss ways and laws have cost me a few times when I failed to recycle something that could have been recycled or did my laundry on a day that was not the day assigned to me. Everything was so regulated that each apartment in my building was given a day and time to do their laundry, and I often sneaked down and did laundry when I could fit it into my schedule. You can't throw anything away that could be recycled or you get fined. If you use the wrong trash bag, they somehow track you down and put the trash and a fine back on your door step. At least there was order—if only I knew all the rules! But overall, I appreciate the cleanliness, orderliness, and punctuality of the Swiss. I also enjoyed their safe public transportation and grocery stores. And it didn't hurt that I lived near and could run past the Nestle factory and can have all the cheese I want. My running route was a trail that goes all the way around a lake in perhaps the most beautiful scenery I have ever seen. One side of the lake is a beautiful mountainside with wildflowers everywhere with a dirt trail running along the edge of the lake. The other side of the lake was a gorgeous Swiss village. I also found time during my lunch break to sneak away from school and put in a few miles—occasionally even joined by one of the students, Tina. My heel spurs had healed with a few months of rest.

There was a lot less adjusting that needs to be done to the culture than in Bulgaria. I think the only real adjustment was that everything had a place, a time, and a purpose. I got overwhelmed once in a while by the abundance of stuff, compared to Bulgaria. I mean, there are several types of cereal to choose from instead of only being able to find cereal once in a while. I also learned that if I attempted to speak the German, they would rescue me in English. I started taking German classes at the local Migros market—sort of an all-in-one grocery store. And any every chance I got, I sat in on the beginning German class at school.

I was also able to travel around Europe on the weekends in my little Fiat Uno. I went to Salzburg, Austria, where I took the Sound of Music Tour twice. Perhaps I should have spent the summer working at the school there! And oh, how romantic the castles are in Vienna—if only I would have had someone special to share it with. I went to Munich, Germany, several times, and visited Auschwitz, the concentration camp. I even went to Paris for a long weekend. Zurich is so centrally located in Europe that the high-speed trains make about any destination reachable in a weekend.

To top it all off, my family came over to spend Christmas and New Year's with me. I will never forget going to the Christmas Eve service at Grossmunster Cathedral in downtown Zurich, as we were joined by Jeff, my key volunteer leader. It was beautiful inside this famous church, and we went up to the balcony so my family could really experience the Swiss culture. The only problem was that the entire service was in German, and once again, we did not speak German. So after about thirty minutes, we decided to leave and tried to sneak out through the abbey. Unbeknownst to us, once we entered the abbey, the doors locked behind us! We were locked inside the courtyard, where the rain began to fall. Finally we found our way out, bought two umbrellas from a gypsy woman outside the church, and headed out for a spaghetti dinner.

The day after Christmas, we rented a van and drove throughout Germany, Switzerland, and Italy. It was so nice to be with my family and show them Europe. My dad loved the beer in Germany, and my younger brother Lucas, who turned eighteen while we were in Germany, also got to have some beer. My older brother Justin fell in love with the art and architecture in Italy, and my mom loved the Swiss ski chalet. I have never appreciated family vacations so much until this moment; I was going to cherish this moment in my heart forever.

I began the new year by making five goals for myself:

Goals for 1996

1.   To remain above reproach in my character.

2.   To allow my love to flow more freely.

3.   To commit to spending ten minutes a day in prayer.

4.   To treat each student as an individual.

5.   To run a marathon.

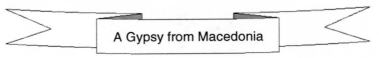

A Gypsy from Macedonia

Every teacher develops favorite students each year. For whatever reason, you get closer to some students than you do others. One student I got close to was a young man named Manuel, a gypsy from

Macedonia. He intrigued me. I had never known a gypsy, and I really didn't even know what that term meant. He would stay after class with a few other boys. One day, we went outside and shot baskets when he began to tell me about his life—the life of a gypsy boy. I could understand a little of what he described, because gypsies were common in Bulgaria. Thank You, Lord, that I had a point of reference to understand him. He was raised in a tent village, and every day, he was to steal as much as possible while roaming the streets. They would travel throughout Macedonia and other countries, living off of everyone else. Manuel's mother had the wisdom to know that she wanted a better life for Manuel, so she sent him to Switzerland to live with an "uncle." He found his way to our private school through an organization set up by George Soros to take Eastern European students and teach them about democracy and then send them back home. Seeing that George Soros is one of the richest men in the world, he found the money to let Manuel attend our school. He was such a humble boy and so eager to learn.

Jan. 18, 1996

> *Yesterday was one of the single hardest days I've ever had to go through. Manuel, who is such a kind-hearted young man, was forced to leave the country because he is a refugee. They actually came to our school and physically took him away. He must go back to Scopia, Macedonia, and live in a gypsy village. Life doesn't seem fair to him. He is so assimilated to the Western world now that it will be very hard on him to return to that lifestyle. Lord, I pray that he would come to know You. You are all he has to rely on.*

Jan. 29, 1996

> *As the Romani trip gets closer, I pray for protection, participation, funds, and that the kids' hearts would be prepared. God, You have placed it on my heart that Manuel is to join us in Romania. Father, how can I make this happen? Lord, I pray for a location for the Battle of the Bands so we can raise the money and raise interest in Romania.*

School was back in full swing, and I found it hard to balance full-time ministry and full-time teaching. One great part of the teaching job was that as a part of our PE program, we go skiing every Tuesday, and the school would pay for it. Fortunately (or unfortunately), I was one of the better skiers on the faculty, so it was my responsibility to keep an eye on our top skiers. Needless to say, I couldn't keep up. In addition to skiing with the top students, I had been convinced to coach the boys' varsity high school basketball team. Never in my wildest dreams would I ever coach boys' *anything.* There were so many international schools in Switzerland that, unlike Bulgaria, we didn't have to leave the country to find competition.

Feb. 5, 1996

> *So many thoughts are rushing through my head. I am dealing with "top executive" type people and I am not used to that. Jeff wants to sit down and help me become more organized. This will be a good thing for me. Don't become offended! People are calling out for direction, and I am not able to direct. I pray that this weekend in Geneva will provide some of that direction for me. I pray that they would send another staff person her to help me.*

Lord, may You hear my prayer and provide a full-time staff person. Lord, give me wisdom and guidance.

School is going much better this semester. The kids and I have settled down. I pray for more Christian fellowship around Zug. Diane Kennedy has been a great friend, and I am so thankful for her.

The snow has come again, and the cold has returned. I have skied more this year already than the last several years combined. My legs are stronger than ever, and my running is going well. I should be prepared for the Torino, Italy, marathon.

God is so good. I could never have imagined a year again when struggling so much in Bulgaria that I would be singing the sound of music on top of the Swiss Alps and really loving life. I was now able to understand some of what God did in my heart last year in stripping away so many fears and insecurities and to accept His love and blessings for me. And I now realize that He can and will use me no matter how inadequate I may feel if I let Him.

CHAPTER 6

Romania (and Oh So Much More)

In preparation for our two-week service project to Romania, the Young Life groups from Düsseldorf, Frankfurt, Munich, and Zurich all came to join with Youth for Christ Geneva in Geneva, Switzerland, to plan the trip. Even more exciting was that we agreed to have J.C. Bowman come over as the camp speaker. It is always so encouraging to spend time with him.

I got in a twenty-one-mile run today, and yet I find it difficult to get motivated. I must remain dedicated. My diet has gotten bad; I must work on healthier eating habits.

Mar. 1, 1996

Lord, You are a mighty God. After speaking at the American International School of Zurich (AISZ) assembly, five girls immediately signed up to go to Romania. Then I learned that last night, people at our church were praying for us. I must spend more time in prayer. Why am I struggling in my prayer life? God is being so faithful. Am I deserving of it?

As I look back a year ago, I am struck by what God has taught me, how much my situation has changed,

and how much growing I still have to do. My Lenten
commitment has not been very strong. What am I
thinking? Why do I fall back spiritually when things are
running smoothly? PRAY! PRAY! PRAY!

Just when I thought it was going to be easy to get the kids to
agree to go to Romania, Satan attacked. One young lady, who is a
Christian, thought that Young Life was a cult and started telling
everyone not to go. I needed to take Pastor Scott with me to talk with
her and her parents before everyone backed out.

Mar. 14, 1996

I come before You, Lord, with so many anxious
thoughts. Raising enough money for the trip to Romania,
get students to sign up to go to Romania, and Manuel in
Macedonia. I give these to You and I know if it is Your
will it will be done. My heart for Manuel continues to
grow. It would be wonderful to see him again and have
another chance to share the gospel with him. We are only
two and a half weeks away from our departure. Lord,
open the minds and hearts of those going that they may
see You.

I can't sort out my feelings toward my singleness.
Father, You have my husband picked out for me and I
know when we are both ready, we will meet. And may
I really believe what I just wrote! May I continue to be
formed into a woman of God.

There is less than a week to go before our service project
to Romania. Securing visas for the non-American kids was an
unexpected challenge. We have to drive across several borders and

non-Americans and non-EU members need visas. Over the weekend, we held the first annual Battle of the Bands competition. The idea came from the Youth for Christ group in Geneva that they had done something similar as a fundraiser and had a great turnout. We found this great little underground venue that the kids really thought was great. We had bands from both International Schools. It was a fabulous event; eighty-three kids and eleven leaders showed up. Even some parents came to check things out. Because of the event, we raised enough money for everyone to go. Praise God.

Mar. 26, 1996

> *A verse in I Samuel, "speak, Lord, for Your servant is listening" has been coming to me often. I wonder if I really am listening to God. When do I give Him time to be able to hear Him? We must pray a prayer of protection over us as we travel to Romania.*

Lugoj, Romania

Great news! It was a total God thing. Somehow through the George Soros Foundation, I was able to get in touch with Manuel in Macedonia. We arranged to pick him up in Budapest, Hungary, so he can join us in Romania. I had to wire money to the foundation's office, and they tracked him down and bought him a train ticket. Praise God.

I was so excited to see him and have another chance to share God's love with him. But the moment I saw him, I knew he was a different boy. His face looked worn and weathered. He had aged and lost that boyish enthusiasm. It was very difficult for his friends, who were so excited to see him and now deal with how much he had changed. I should have been more prepared for that, but I wasn't.

We arrived in Lugoj, Romania, and God's hand carried us through many borders. I am so thankful for all the people lifting us up in prayer as we traveled. We spent a total of three hours at the borders and had to buy only one visa. God most definitely paved the way for us, because there were a few kids on the bus who did not obtain the correct visa yet were allowed to pass.

Apr. 3, 1996

> *So many thought are running through my head—
> thoughts of Bulgaria, orphans, lost souls, a hurting
> and dying world. My heart aches thinking about these
> orphans. Lord, thank You for bringing Manuel here with
> us. I know that You are going to work mightily on his
> heart.*
>
> *My prayer for the Christian kids, Lord, is that they
> would see how Christlike they can be by serving You in the
> mission field. My prayer for the unsaved is that they would
> come to know and accept You as Lord and Savior.*

Our living conditions are much better than I had anticipated. I guess my time in Bulgaria was great preparation for these two weeks. The quality was a big morale booster for the group, as we had prepared them for the worst. Our goal initially had been to build an orphanage. However, as we saw the floor plans, plus the tools and equipment we had, matched with the size of the group, we realized this will not happen. Our days were spent digging and digging and digging. We had to dig the foundation and all we had were shovels. It would take a truck in the States one day to do what fifty of us accomplished in two weeks. I guess the blessing in it all was that being stuck in the trenches with someone is very conducive for learning about their lives and sharing yours. We also had some very interesting conversations because of the mixing of the group. We had an Australian girl, two Indian kids, a Japanese boy, two Spanish girls, several Germans and Americans, and a few French. Often what you thought you heard was nothing close to what was actually said and this led to some hysterical moments at the bottom of a hole.

At night, we held a sort of traditional Young Life club. JC is doing a great job of sharing the gospel to the kids and we have amazing discussions back in our room afterward. Each day as we continue digging, they are so full of questions about the message, the Bible, and Jesus. The Lord's presence is very strong.

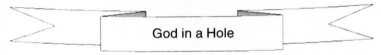

God in a Hole

Luckily, one of the volunteer leaders from Munich was a nurse who was very good at bandaging blisters. After one week of digging, our hands and muscles were ready for a break. We decided to do something very different for our Easter service. We got everyone up just as the sun was rising and we went for a walk. The kids had no idea where we were going, so when we ended up at a cemetery, I think they thought we had lost our minds. JC then talked about death and explained how Jesus died on the cross for them. It was a very powerful message that I know will be with the kids for a lifetime. We then sang a few songs and walked back to our campsite for what had become our typical breakfast—stale Froot Loops and pickles. We didn't have the heart to tell the wonderful Romanian women who had volunteered to cook for us for the two weeks—and were so proud of the fact that they had bought us American cereal—that the food was awful. We never did figure out why they served us pickles.

I was very discouraged by what I saw in Manuel. He was guarding his heart and not wanting to participate in the discussions. I could see the pain in his face, as once again he would have to leave us and go back to his gypsy life while we went back to the comforts of Zurich. I didn't know how to help him—Lord, I lift him up to *You*.

Apr. 7, 1996

Here I am in Lugoj, Romania, on Easter day. The sun is shining, and we are resting on the Sabbath. This seems a far cry from the Holy Land Easter I had last year. The one good thing about the food here is that I like the coffee!

The kids are great. They are working so hard and really paying attention at night. Lord, may You continue to reveal Yourself to Georgina, Manuel, Caroline, Masato, Jeff, Aaron, Jincy, and Joyal. The time that I have been able to spend with them alone in a hole digging is incredible. It may be a difficult transition when we get back to being their teacher and not just their friend.

As I reflect back on a year ago, I realize how much You have taught me in a year about the person that You want me to become. It's never fun learning a lesson until you are able to look back and see what you have learned and how you have grown from it. Lord, thank You for the lesson in Bulgaria last year. Thank You for loving me so much that You wouldn't let me stay in my comfort zone in Colorado.

*My energy level is high, Lord, and I pray that my
strength, patience, and wisdom continue. I must lift my
cares to You and let You carry them.*

The second-to-last night in Romania, we performed a Young Life tradition. We asked the students who had decided to give their lives to Jesus Christ to stand up and say so. Several of the students did stand up and shared that they wanted Jesus as their Lord and Savior. We knew the angels in heaven were rejoicing.

We even had a surprise as Masato, a junior boy who was half-Swiss and half-Japanese, stood up. His father was actually the Japanese ambassador to Switzerland. I had no idea what he was going to say, because he was such a reserved young man and I did not get to know him as well as the others. As he stood up, he said that the night before we were to leave for Romania, he had decided to end his life. He was going to slit his wrists while lying in the bathtub. The pain was not a deterrent, as this was a boy who had two teeth pulled while living in Saudi Arabia, without any Novocain or painkiller. You could sort of hear this collective gasp as he shared that with us.

He went on to say that just as he was about to slit his wrists, he decided that he would do one last "nice" thing for this world before leaving it. He explained that he would go to Romania, build this school for the orphans, and then take his life. As the tears welled up in his eyes as well as the eyes of everyone in the room, he said, "I did lose my life today. I gave it to Jesus." He said, "If Jesus was willing to die such a horrible death for me, then surely I could live a magnificent life for Him." He told us about this joy that was now in his heart that took his pain away. He even started giggling as he told us about this great joy. Ending his life was no longer an option as he wanted to live the abundant life that Christ had promised him.

What an amazing moment that was for all of us. And it wasn't just talk. When we got back to Zurich, Masato was a different person. The entire faculty at school kept on asking me what we did to him because he couldn't stop grinning from ear to ear. And when they asked Masato directly he was prepared with an answer that would stop even the staunchest atheist.

I had arranged with Manuel a way to continue communications with him. When we dropped him off at the bus station in Budapest, Hungary, on our way home, my heart broke for him.

I never heard from Manuel again.

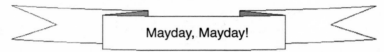

Mayday, Mayday!

May 4, 1996

> *Ever since returning from Romania, I have had this unmotivated feeling in my heart. Maybe apathetic is a better word. The Lord did so many wonderful things in the lives of kids and leaders. Why do I feel so blah? Perhaps it is because of how little time I have spent with the Lord in the past month. Plus I always seem to get the May "blues" at school.*

> *I am feeling a bit lonely and am longing for a special relationship. I think that is why I am putting so much thought and energy into dreaming about my future husband. Why am I crying? I can't stop thinking about all I went through and learned last year. Why is my memory so short though? I am quickly back to my selfish behavior. Why do I think that I can live without giving*

every aspect of my life into the Lord's hands? I would
rather He was in control—but my grip is strong!

I was so close! My goal was to run under four hours but I finished the Turino (Italy) Marathon in 4:05! I beat my old time by three minutes, but still, what a bummer. Oh well, I did feel much better after this marathon than the last one I ran, even though it rained during the entire race. The blisters on my feet were huge, because of the friction with the wet socks, but overall, they were nothing serious. There were no big epiphanies like during the race in San Francisco. In fact, the only thing I thought about was Dean Martin. My good friends Di and Steve drove me to the race and Di—being the thoughtful person she was—put Dean Martin's "That's Amore" on the cassette. Now a little pizza in your eye isn't too bad, but to have that song running through your head for four hours and only know that one line, "When the moon hits your eye like a big pizza pie, that's amore!" just about did me in!

May 17, 1996

> *My soul is searching. Why am I here? Am I making*
> *a difference? Am I allowing God to use me and work*
> *through me? Is my selfishness controlling me? Once*
> *again, I feel like I cannot do this anymore. Who am I*
> *that these kids should listen to me? I need help, guidance,*
> *Christian brothers and sisters.*

> *I am feeling a bit lonely as well. I realize that no guys*
> *here are the one that I want to spend my life with. Lord,*
> *how much longer must I wait? When will I be ready for*
> *that type of a relationship? Will I ever be ready? I pray*
> *that the man You have for me Lord has a greater love*
> *for You than anything else on this earth. I pray the same*

thing for myself. But I feel too young, too inexperienced, too selfish right now. "People say that I'm amazing, strong beyond my years. But they don't see the enemy that lays me on my knees. And they don't know that I go running home when I fall down. They don't know who picks me up when no one is around. I drop my sword and cry for just a while. 'cause deep inside this armor, this warrior is a child." Twila Paris This Warrior is a Child Amen

Sue Bates, one of the Young Life Interns in Geneva, came up for the weekend. We had discussions about her joining me next year. It is very hard to teach full time and do Young Life full time. I fear that my teaching was suffering, and I didn't want to give the kids anything less than my best. I needed to keep teaching for my visa to live here and so I could have enough money to live on.

May 28, 1996

It's Justin's birthday again. Thank You, Lord, for giving us another year with him. I hope he enjoys the Parisian painting I sent to him.

At times, it is so hard to be joyful in all occasions. I am really struggling with moral issues at the International School. I feel that we are trying to be too open, too self-guiding, and are modeling immoral lives. I don't know how much longer I can teach in this setting. Oh, but that is probably why the Lord has placed me at this school. You don't build character on the mountaintops, but only in the valleys and deserts! Lord, I pray for our faculty as we seek out a new director.

Here I sit on yet another rainy spring day. The Munich church retreat that I attended in Mittersill, Austria, was a nice getaway. It was so nice not to be in charge of anything and to be ministered to. The Lord was revealing to me how little I give to Him in my daily/hourly decision making. Plus I have realized how my standards/ morals change depending on the culture/friends/job that I am in. Why do I not carry the standards of Jesus with me into those places instead of letting my circumstances dictate my "view" of Jesus' standards?

It seems to be that time of year for personal reflection. My heart had been very troubled lately, and I couldn't figure out why. I was frustrated with the administration at school, and I didn't know if I could work under these same conditions next year. There were some great staff members who had become friends, but the direction the administration was taking doesn't sit well with me. I feel that I am going against my standards—Jesus' standards. Am I just too old-fashioned, even at twenty-five? Is it wrong to be old-fashioned?

As I think about it more, I realize that I am so frustrated because I cannot do both of my jobs to the best of my ability. My gifts (or lack thereof) had really showed through this year. I am horrible at leading a committee and leadership building stuff. It's a sense of relief to recognize my feelings are from my perceived inadequacies and not the circumstances at school. But God had called me there to teach me how to become a better leader of adults? My first reaction is no; I want to work with someone trained in this area. It's just not my fit. How often can I use that as a reason not to do something, though? Is that why I am trying so hard to get another staff person here so that I don't have to be the point person?

May 31, 1996

> *Lord, please bring another staff person to join me so*
> *I don't have to work on my weaknesses. It's too hard. And*
> *Lord, please be preparing me and my future husband for*
> *our meeting and work quickly. I want to start a family. I*
> *am already twenty-five!*

As the school year wrapped up, I was trying to make plans to see the kids over the summer. This past Sunday, Masato, Georgina, and I went to church and showed the Romanian slides. It was well received by the congregation, and many were touched. Masato shared his testimony with them, and I could see so much growth in him.

Saturday was graduation, and our wee little school only had two seniors. It was difficult saying good-bye to all of the kids who are moving. Lord, please place someone in their lives who is willing to share Your love with them. I am having doubts about returning after next year. Should I go back to school? Move back to the United States and teach? Go to another country with Young Life? Lord, as I begin to look forward, may I listen for Your guiding words, yet live every day for the moment. I pray that as I head back to the United States for the summer that I gain clarity about my future.

Jun. 10, 1996

> *Once again, I am on one of my non-eating days,*
> *trying to master my stomach. There has to be a better way*
> *to suppress and control my appetite and binges. Lord, I*
> *cannot do this without You. I have tried. Jesus, may Your*
> *prayer become mine. "My food," said Jesus, "is to do*
> *the will of Him who sent me and to finish His work (John*
> *4:34)." Lord, help me to see food in this way.*

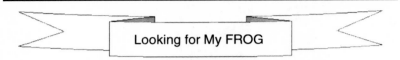

Looking for My FROG

After spending the last two weeks of June with my family, I headed to Colorado Springs, where I have decided to take classes at Fuller Theological Seminary. I was very excited to be around like-minded people, study the Word, and perhaps even meet someone special. This someone special had come to be known among my friends as my FROG, my "Friendly Righteous Outgoing Guy." I was looking for a FROG who would turn into a prince and sweep me off my feet. On the second day of class, I was intrigued by sitting on the other side of the desk and being the student instead of the teacher. Perhaps this is a sign that I should go back to school. We really enjoy learning and thinking critically. I could consider a Christian counseling or social work degree.

My spiritual life had been very dry lately. Why am I not spending time with the Lord? It was so comfortable being home that my time is unfocused. Lord, may following You become my vocation. I had felt very inadequate in terms of my leadership abilities. God blessed me with so many gifts, but administration is not one of them. Is it my pride that keeps pushing me on? Am I feeling called into full-time Young Life staff? Lord, speak: Your servant is listening. May Your will, not mine, be done.

Jul. 2, 1996

My eagerness to come to Colorado and take a seminary class to meet "new potentials" is gone due to the lack of prospective men. Once again, the Lord has used my poor intentions to draw me toward Him. My desire to be married and partnered in ministry continues to grow. Lord, I know that You have someone

*incredible for me if that is Your will. Is it Your will that
I get married? May I continue to become the woman of
excellence that my future husband is looking for.*

After watching a ninety-minute video on Mother Teresa, the term *incarnational ministry* takes on new meaning. How can I become more incarnate to those teenagers in Zurich? I learned so much from the others during our time outside of class. I played golf with a couple of married men, and it was interesting listening to them talk about marriage. One guy told me that you fall in love with a person after you've been married for a while and the romance is gone. I will have to think about that one for a while. Another friend said that you need to fall in love with Jesus in someone. That sounds like the perfect relationship, where this man would fall in love with the Jesus in me.

As class drew to a close, I managed to talk three of my friends from back home into joining me in a European adventure. We spent three weeks taking the train through Switzerland, German, Italy, and France. It was so much fun. We even went to the prince of Monte Carlo's house. We stood at his gates yelling up at his castle and asking him if he was our frog—if we kissed him, would he turn into our prince? Unfortunately he never came outside. It was the perfect end to the summer, and the last three days were spent sitting at the beach in Nice, France, taking in the ambiance that France has to offer. I was refreshed and ready for another school year in Zurich. Look out, kids, the Feather is back!

CHAPTER 7

God, I Want to Go Home

It rained nonstop since my return to Switzerland. Very few of my friends were here and it had been lonely. I tended to sleep more and eat more. I had gotten some good reading in, though, especially Matthew chapter 4, about what it takes to be a disciple of Jesus. I realized that my loneliness here was for Him. Unlike Jesus, I gave in to the many temptations of the world. "Holy Spirit, give me the strength to withstand temptations." I prayed for a "Holy Spirit Experience" as Jim Rayburn, the founder of Young Life, called it. God has placed Himself in me, yet I do not look to the Holy Spirit for strength. What a fool I am. My pride and determination get in the way many times of what I could actually be doing. If only I let God take over! I must increase my prayer life. Lord, teach me how to meditate on Your love. "Search me, O God, and know my heart; test me and know my anxious thoughts. See if there is any offensive way in me and lead me in the way everlasting." Psalm 139:23&24.

My new place was along Lake Zurich in a town called Thalwil. It was very spacious and light, with a view of the lake. It was a far cry from the "Heidi House" on the mountaintop. I could actually walk to the train and grocery store. School started just where it left off, but my class load was lighter. I prayed that I could be a light in a dark place.

One young man named Zander was new this year. He had moved eleven times in the past seven school years. He had been beaten so badly that he could only write on a computer. There had been so much brain and nerve damage that he had lost most of his control of his hands. Another kid, named Phillip, had a father who was so wealthy that he would buy Phillip anything he wanted, yet wouldn't spend one minute with him. Sophie had to live with her mother, father, and his girlfriend. And Paul was being forced to take over his father's multimillion-dollar company—and he wanted nothing to do with it. Lord, parenting is such a responsibility! How can I teach kids about a loving father when they do not have one?

Sept. 20, 1996

There has been a bit of a scare with my brother Justin. It is so hard after ten years of remission, realizing that his cancer could come back. Lord, I pray that he would continually look to You and surrender daily to You. He has such a kind and joyful spirit.

Father, I thank You for Lucas's happiness and success. It is great having e-mail contact with him. I am so proud of him.

I pray, Lord, that I would be able to spend more time with kids this year. For it is in our friendship that they will see You. Thank You for the work that You are doing in Georgina. My heart is filled with joy and peace this morning and I love You, Lord!

My thoughts whirled around in my head as I reflected on the last couple of days. I tried so hard to help a student several times, only to have her mother attack me. I didn't want to come off as a threat to her mom, but there was something very unhealthy going on in her home. Why is it that those who require the most energy don't see how I will bend over backwards for them? I have learned a great deal about communication with parents.

The cool thing at school was to starve oneself—and be nasty to others. Lord, so many of these kids are hurting so badly. Then, to top it all off, the faculty was very unhappy about salaries. Yet amid all this chaos, I was able to spend more time in the Word, studying and memorizing Scriptures. It was comforting to know that we have a God we can cast all our anxieties on because He cares for us. The plans for a full-time Young Life person to join or replace me in Zurich continued on. Lord, my vision/method for establishing an International School ministry seemed to be successful. Is this what You are calling me to do? Is it Your will that I become the community prep person who gets the areas ready for the permanent full-time staff person?

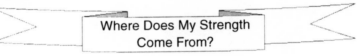

Where Does My Strength Come From?

Oct. 3, 1996

> *As my desire to leave this school grows, I lay this decision at Your feet, Lord. May my heart and ears be open to hear Your calling. Lord, thanks for such a beautiful new flat and for providing a wonderful roommate.*

The last couple of weeks had been crazy. My dad came over and we had a great time. We went to Innsbruck and Salzburg, Austria; Prague, Czech Republic; and Berlin and Munich, Germany, all during my fall break. We would wake up early each morning and run through the city streets before breakfast. This was a great way to explore a new city and spend super quality time with my dad.

Most of my efforts had been focused on getting a full-time staff person here. When I stop and think about how far the ministry has come in a little over a year, I am brought to my knees; I realize how little of it I have actually done. God was working here. Young Life HQ approached me about moving to Hong Kong and becoming the area director there. I was definitely entertaining the thought. I believed it would be a church partnership. There were nine international schools and over twelve thousand international teens there. They would like to turn it into the Asian HQ. Yet I was afraid of committing to living another two years overseas. I sent out my application to stateside regional directors with Young life and the London Recruiting Fair. My fear was that my selfish desires blocked out what the Lord was saying.

Oct. 26, 1996

>*I've come to the desert as far as men are concerned. I am writing to a few guys I've met but . . . Why can't I ever get past the "big brother" syndrome? My desires to be married and have a family are strong these days. I would love to be working/ministering internationally with my husband.*

>*I've been spending the time in the car each morning memorizing Scripture. That is such a great way to grow for me.*

It was amazing how quickly the year passed. It had been a difficult fall in terms of spiritual battles. But the Holy Spirit was alive and working overtime. One of the most humbling and encouraging things happened that week. My good friend Di, who had struggled with her relationships to guys and her mother, asked me if my strength was in my own nature or spiritual. She said that there was a strength about me that she was attracted to. I shared with her that my strength was found in the Lord and Him only. It was an incredible experience, and I was looking forward to spending time with her in Kenya over Christmas. We had a great trip planned.

A student of mine named Olivia had been my major priority. Her mother was dying of liver cancer and her stepmom had passed away the previous year. The Lord had given me some wonderful opportunities to spend time with her and share my faith with her. Lord, I pray that You would comfort her in her loss and may she come to accept Your love. At just thirteen, it was very hard for her to understand why two such important women in her life had been touched by cancer. It was hard for me to understand this too.

Nov. 5, 1996

Personally, I am confused on what avenues I should be perusing for next year: stay here, go to the States, seek out a church partnership in Hong Kong or another country as a teacher. Lord, may my heart hear Your words, may my heart and mind follow Your call. When You called my name, I didn't know how far the calling went!

Would I be willing to stay here if I were married? Probably. Is my singleness and desire for a husband so great that I am not open to hearing God's call? I think that a fear of loneliness and singleness are huge factors. Lord, how do I give those up to You? If I say okay, I will stay and it's okay if I don't get married then I can't expect You to turn around and say, "Since you were faithful and gave it up—here's a husband." I must fully be ready to give that up! I don't know if I can do that.

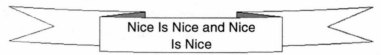

Nice Is Nice and Nice Is Nice

I felt like my work here was done and the road was paved for someone else to begin working here. I didn't feel one way or another about me being that full-time person and quitting teaching. I looked at many different options and my prayer was that my selfishness was not the guiding force, but that God was. Lord, how do I find the way? When I asked God to show me the way, His response to me was, "I am the way and if you are walking with Me, you will not lose your way."

Nov. 22, 1996

To pray is to descend with the mind into the heart and there to stand before the face of the Lord, ever-present, all seeing, within you."

—Theophan the Recluse, a Russian mystic

"When we learn to descend with our mind into our heart, then all those who have become part of our life are led into the healing presence of God and touched by him in the center of our being. We are speaking here about the mystery for which words are inadequate. It is the mystery that the heart, which is the center of our being, is transformed by God into His own heart, a heart large enough to embrace the entire universe. Through prayer, we can carry in our heart all human pain and sorrow, all conflicts and agonies, all torture and war, all hunger, loneliness, and misery, not because of some

great psychological or emotional capacity, but because
God's heart has become one with ours."

—The Ways of the Heart
Henri J.M. Nowen

This is what my soul longs for: a heart that is one
with God's!

As I sit here on the shore of the Mediterranean in Nice, France, I read about the Prodigal Son. As I contemplate which role I feel best fits me, the man next to me prays to Mohammad. The people all around me worship money, fame, and alcohol. I feel like I ran away from home to experience the world, but I don't like what the world has to offer—greed, loneliness, pain, hunger, and war. How do I go back home? Oh Lord, I want to go home and be with You! Lord, how do I live a life where my mind and heart become Your heart? I want so much to experience Your peace, Your love, Your joy, and Your acceptance. Lord, please hear the cries of my heart and show me the way.

Nov. 24, 1996

I am afraid that Pastor Scott may be right when he
said that my desire to go back to the US is to get married.
I do feel that as long as I am overseas, I will never meet
my husband. I'd hoped that my faith and judgment were
above that influence—guess I was wrong!

Thanksgiving was great this year. No fancy or exotic trips, but I did get a visit from an old high school friend. My friend, Guy, who was my basketball buddy in high school and was now modeling underwear in Milan, came up for a visit. I have never before had this experience where the man I was walking down the street with was so good-looking that both men and women stared at him. It was nice to see Guy again, but the life he lived seemed far from anything good. He even admitted that it was the devil's industry. I just prayed that he would be drawn to God as he faced his fears and loneliness.

The snow came down in buckets the last couple of days. I was not ready for winter to arrive. I was very excited about my Christmas trip to Kenya with Di. Last night, we had to cancel our Young Life scavenger hunt because no one was going to come. It made me realize that no one will come to us—we have to go to them. Lord, it's so hard to get these leaders to go to a kid event. Please make it possible for a full-time person to come over here for next year. There is so much contact work to be done and kids to love. Father, I am so uncertain still about my next step. A part of me wants to flee Switzerland, and the other part feels there are kids here that it would be hard to leave. Lord, mold me and make me into a child of God who will go recklessly into the world, preaching the gospel.

Dec. 22, 1996

It was wonderful talking to Lucas on his birthday yesterday. My excitement for Kenya is so strong, yet I am really going to miss spending the holidays with my family. I have been writing Christmas cards and repeating one phrase on every card. "May you meet the Prince of Peace in a fresh and new way this season." Maybe that is what my soul is yearning for: the Prince of Peace.

My anxieties over Justin continue to grow. Lord, I don't even know how to pray for him. I love him so very

deeply. Lord, may he be drawn closer to You each and
every day. Protect him from the seizures.

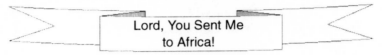

Lord, You Sent Me
to Africa!

We arrived in Kenya on December 23 and were greeted by the sun—what a blessing. We spent our first day at the pool and beach at the Silver Star Hotel in Mombasa, Kenya. It was so nice to relax and soak up some rays. The flight over was okay, but it was the most uncomfortable I have ever been on a plane. Di and I were stuck in the last row with smokers, and our seats would not recline. The entire nine-hour flight, we had to sit upright. At least the plane ride had a pit stop in Luxor, Egypt—we didn't get to see anything, but at least I can add that to places I have been. The people at the resort were very friendly, and so far the food was okay. The Indian Ocean was very beautiful and warm. I made the mistake of getting up early and leaving the protection of our resort to go for a run into the city of Mombasa. The Muslim men did not take kindly to a western woman wearing short running shorts and a T-shirt running through their streets. They yelled and whistled at me, but not in a way the indicated pleasure. Rather, it was distaste.

Dec. 23 1996

I was able to spend some time in prayer during the
flight and at the pool. It's hard being away from family. Di
is having a very difficult time in her life. Lord, only You
can fill the hole in her heart. May You speak through me
this trip. I hope that I can find a church to attend tomorrow
night. As I lay my head down and my sun-soaked body to
rest, I say a special prayer for my family.

On Christmas Eve, we snorkeled, swam, played water polo, and even saw a native dance show. The place really was paradise. I had some fun bargaining for souvenirs. Even literally gave the shirt off my back in exchange for an elephant carved out of wood. Di, on the other hand, paid through the nose for the same things. The people here really tried to make this a nice resort. My heart, however, was not at ease. This was such a country of rich and poor. Lord, how are many of these people ever going to hear about Your love? The man at the hotel change shop was a Christian and shared a bit. So much energy and passion went into his speech from his heart. Lord, I want to have that same passion.

It did not seem like Christmas Eve at all. This was the first and hopefully last time that I was unable to attend a church service on this night. It was comforting to think of the routine that my family was going through this night. My childhood routine. I knew they were meeting with all their friends before church for pizza. Then, they would go to church and then the party at the Watsons' before heading home to bed. Being here with Di had been difficult, because I had not been able to share all the feelings in my heart. Lord, I pray that I will be open and available for You on the upcoming safari. This is such an incredible Earth You created. As I studied the "coral niche" today, I was taken by the details you took such care in providing even the under the sea. Such magnificent colors and beauty,

Dec. 24, 1996

As I prepare for bed here in Mombasa, I long to be with You, Lord. This must have been such a difficult night for you 2,000 years ago. Please, Lord, be with those I love and am missing right now. May they feel Your presence and know that I am thinking of them. Father, I lift up a special thank-you for Justin; the way You have

used his life to reach so many. Lord, thank You also for
the birth of Your Son and for making Him my Savior and
that I am now Your child.

My first Christmas in the sun! I was feeling very lonely for other Christians today until I got to Nairobi. It was wonderful to see everyone walking the streets in their Sunday best. There were many churches there, and Christian music played everywhere. I had such a great quiet time in the car. I felt God's presence as we drove. The Holy Spirit was alive in my heart, and I felt in communion with Him. What an awesome God I serve.

I've enjoyed haggling and purchased some nice gifts. I wish my family could see all of this. I have fallen in love with the little African children, and my desire for my own family grows. I made a promise with God that if He called me to Africa, I would go. I really feel like someday I may end up here. I can't believe it myself. As for today, I am enjoying God's creation. We saw many domestic animals, and banana, pineapple, and coffee fields. Tomorrow, the real safari begins.

Dec. 25, 1996

It's been a tough day spiritually with Di. She has
become sarcastic about religion. Perhaps that is her
defense to the Holy Spirit knocking on her heart. The Mt.
Kenya resort is beautiful. It has rained a lot and we have
a fire going. Last night, it was the AC; tonight, a fire.

We arrived at the Samburu Game Preserve. We saw elephants, giraffes, lions, zebras, gazelles, dik-diks, and a leopard. I was three feet away from a lion. We were chased by a mad elephant and surrounded by a herd of giraffes. All I can say about this place is "awesome!" We met some Sambu natives. They live on meat, milk, and blood. They are related to the Masai, and cover themselves in blood as part of their attire.

As we continued on from park to park, we were amazed at what we saw. We were on our fourth day of safari and we saw twenty little lion cubs. Yesterday we saw rhinos and the king of the jungle. He put on a little mating show for us—and if were to return in six months, we might see the results. Yet I got frustrated with my driver, who was very persistent about being next to me. He was making me nervous. The two other couples on our tour were very Swiss! I kept seeing lots of kids, and Di said I've got the fever for them. The more I travel and see, the more I wish I had my own family to share it with.

Dec. 29, 1996

> *I don't think I have ever had the marriage urge as strong as it is now. Lord, if it's Your will, I would love to love a man and get married. I'm trying to be patient as You prepare the two of us. Father, please forgive me for my thoughts about Di. It is hard being around someone who rejects all that You are about. She is such a good friend and good person. I thank You, Lord, for being my King, and I pray Psalm 139 to you.*

New Year's Resolutions

It's so hard to believe that it is a new year already. As I looked back at my goals for '96, I saw that I did accomplish some but not all of them. Spending the last two weeks in Kenya helped me to see the world again. Switzerland can put a mask over the poverty in the world. I felt more at home in Kenya than I ever had in Switzerland.

So much had been accomplished here in Zurich, yet I didn't feel that I had been as effective as I could be. Perhaps that was because of the size and nature of my school. I felt that I would be making some major decisions in my life over the next couple of months—all I wanted was to be where God wanted me to be. I had grown a lot in one year. I became more organized, more experienced, and more confident in my public speaking abilities. I could articulate the vision of Young Life much clearer. These were all good things, but was any of it for spiritual gain? Had I become so concerned with the "polish" that I let the inside stay untreated? As I worked through the Bible study, *Experiencing God* by Henry Blackaby, I came to the conclusion that my prayer life was horrific. May I become a woman of prayer this year.

I shared with Di something that I had never shared before but was an underlying motivation in my life. My whole life, I have succeeded in whatever I have tried—in school, sports, and friends I have been very dependent on my own abilities. Now I have reached a stage where no matter how "good" I am, it will not be good enough. Now I must step beyond myself, realize my human limitations, and give it all up to God! This was a hard thing for an independent and selfish person to admit.

Goals for 1997

1. To make prayer the priority in my life.

2. To give of my time, my money, my resources, and my prayers. Put others' needs first.

3. To work on communication at school, with friends, family, and God.

4. To run a marathon.

I got very sick with both the flu and a cold. My head had so much pressure built up that it felt like it would explode. It made me think about how much I worship running, since I couldn't run, and that made me more miserable. I watched an interview with the Rev. Billy Graham, and I could feel the presence of the Lord as He spoke. I have found an inner calm and peace about next year and am now trying to focus on the here and now.

Jan. 22, 1997

> *There is no way that this two-week service project to a Croatian refugee site will happen or affect kids lives unless I give it to the Lord. So Father, I lift every last detail up to You. Lord Jesus, may You bring forth those kids whom You are preparing. Take away the fear from their mothers about going to Croatia.*

As the days go by, I realize more and more that I want to try full-time ministry and stop teaching. My heart is not in the teaching, and my students deserve better.

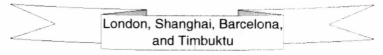

London, Shanghai, Barcelona, and Timbuktu

I decided to go to the European Council of International Schools Job Fair in London, just to keep my options open. There were opportunities in schools in Frankfurt, London, and Shanghai, but only one seemed right—Shanghai. God has revealed how He is working and how I can join Him there. I have met or heard of many Christians who were either in or headed to Shanghai, even other international schoolteachers.

I stayed over a few extra days and my mom flew over to join me. We had such a great time exploring London. We went to two musicals a day. Our last day there, we decided to use the money we would have spent on a final show and have a nice dinner, since we had already seen seven shows in four days.

Mar. 13, 1997

> *It's hard to articulate what I am feeling inside. I have this incredible sense of peace, and I have no idea what I will be doing next year. Lord, we have so many special requests as we prepare for Croatia, the site for this year's service project: visa problems, finances, and kids with a lot of pain in their lives. Father, I just thank You for the peace which passes all understanding.*

> *As I reflect upon the last couple of years, I realize how much I have grown. In moving overseas, I have found myself, yet, I am not finished being molded. I look at my lifestyle and all that I have, family, and friends, yet I feel like this is not my home.*

> *As the snow melts, the flowers begin to bloom and the birds sing. I thank You, Lord, for spring and all the life that goes along with it. And as we near Easter and Your death and resurrection, I think of the life You have given me through Your Son's death. I am so unworthy. I am so ungrateful and I am so selfish. Thank You for loving me despite all of this.*

Barcelona, Spain, is a fabulous place to run a marathon. And it's the Olympic course, nonetheless. My training has gone better than the other two marathons, and I know my time will show that improvement. Again, I hoped to beat the four-hour mark. I trained with two of my volunteers, Angie and Teddy Blankenship, and they were going with me to Spain. Teddy Blankenship was going to run with me. An even greater blessing was that Justin had met a woman from Spain, and the two of them would join us in Barcelona for the weekend. I was so excited to see my brother again and so thankful that he was healthy enough to travel—and that he had a serious girlfriend.

The day of the race was perfect running conditions. I had my family there to cheer me on and a partner to run the race with. Our strategy was to not stop at any of the water stations and just drink on the run. Hopefully, between my better training and this race strategy, I could accomplish my goal. Unfortunately, it was my worst time yet: 4:12. I have no idea what happened.

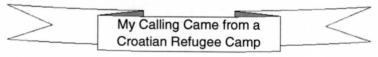

My Calling Came from a
Croatian Refugee Camp

Oh, how quickly my circumstances changed. It appeared that Shanghai was out for next year, but I was amazingly at peace about that. I resigned from the school at the end of the year and had no idea where I should be going. It felt like such a battle going on inside of me. Is discerning God's will supposed to be this hard?

We left for Croatia. The Lord continued to teach me lessons. Jincy, a girl from India who was supposed to join us on the trip, just had her visa denied—at 11:00 AM the day before the trip. Instead of turning to prayer, I began scheming and trying to work any diplomatic connections that I might have. Then, at 2:00 PM, the consulate called and her visa was ready. So many people were praying for her—and I gave up and didn't trust that God would provide when push came to shove.

Mar. 22, 1997

> *As I prepare to leave, I am feeling worn out and depleted. Father, I pray for Your strength to fill me and restore me. Lord, should I go full time with Young Life? Should I stay in teaching? Should I move back to the States? I think that not hearing from Shanghai, the post-marathon blues, and the disappointment of saying good-bye to my brother has all hit me at once.*

> *Take my heart, Lord, take my soul. Lord, I'm begging You to take control of my body and of my mind. Teach me how to leave myself behind.*

Our two weeks in Croatia were very memorable. One young man, Mladen, was able to get together with his grandmother, who lived not far from where we were working. We got through all the borders without any problems. Our goal here in Fuzine, Croatia, was to rebuild refugee housing that had been blown up during the Yugoslavian Revolution. We stayed three blocks away from the worksite where some local women looked after us. One night, we were awakened by a bloodcurdling scream from one of these women. She had just received word that her son had been killed. Until you have been in a war-torn country, you just can't get it. Each day when we walked to our worksite, we were surrounded by woods that we were not allowed to explore because of the undetonated landmines that were planted there.

Unlike last year's trip to Romania, the weather was very cold and snowy. There was a lot of demolition and swinging heavy sledgehammers, fixing roofs and floorboards, and painting. At night, we would listen to T.J Dickerson from Young Life, who came over with his wife. He shared the gospel message. One night after a great message, we were sitting around a bonfire. Olivia, the girl who had just lost her mom to cancer, said, "This has been the best day of my life." God was working in the lives of these kids. One young Jewish girl named Yael learned to love herself and accept love from others on this trip. We even got to see the Hale-Bopp comet flash across the sky. Several of the students asked Christ into their hearts on this trip. On the way home, we spent the night in Venice, Italy, where we all decompressed and showered!

One unexpected blessing I received during the trip was that I finally felt God saying to do ministry full time and stop teaching. Sometimes God has to get you out of your comfort zone in order for you to hear Him. The weather was beautiful in Switzerland, and it seemed like a great place to be. I was shocked to admit it, but in the first couple of days back, I entertained the thought of staying in Zurich for one more year. I was, however, intrigued by the church youth position in Manila and Hong Kong. Boulder, Colorado, also sounded like a great place to be.

Apr. 11, 1997

Tonight is the first annual Young Life banquet in Zurich. Masato and Jincy are sharing their stories. Lord, give them the strength to open up their hearts. Holy Spirit, be at work in the hearts and minds of all those who attend.

After a long meeting with Pastor Scott, I decided to stay overseas. My only reason for returning to the United States was to meet a man and get married. Plus, Pastor Scott shared how when he was in Mexico and struggling with the same thing, the day he told the Lord he would stay in overseas ministry, God brought Kim, his future wife, into his life. Maybe God will bring us together where ever I go next!

Apr. 13, 1997

> *I will sing of the mercies of the Lord forever. With my mouth, I will make your faithfulness known through all generations. I will declare that your love stands firm forever, that you established your faithfulness in heaven itself. (Psalm 89:1-2)*

Lord, Your mercies never end; they are new every morning. Great is their faithfulness. Today, the International Protestant Church voted to join with Young Life in a church partnership. After a very long meeting, the motion was passed. Lord, thank You for being patient with us as we learned to listen to You and step out in faith. Father, I pray for organizational skills during the next couple of months as we prepare for this new Young Life staff person. Give us wisdom and guidance as we begin the process of hiring a person. I am not worthy of being a part of this great work. It has humbled me to a much greater extent than ever before—thank You for that.

CHAPTER 8

From the Alps to the Islands

Go east, young woman, go east. Young Life wanted me to consider Bangkok, Thailand; Hong Kong; Manila, Philippines; or Seoul, South Korea. I have begun to get very sad about leaving Zurich. With only two months left, I want to make the most of my time here. The committee is set, and the churches are on board, so now we pray for God to send a new area director here.

April 21, 1997

Father, can it be that even though I pray for guidance, I am more interested in getting confirmation on where I want to go? Help me, dear Father, to examine my heart. Help me when I pray to have a truly open mind. Today I will spend the day fasting and praying. I give all that I am to you, Lord. May I relinquish all the stresses and burdens to You. For my yoke is heavy. Speak to me, Lord; your servant Angie is listening. "If you remain in me and my words remain in you, ask whatever you wish and it shall be given to you." (John 15:7)

God, why can't I have a burning bush experience instead of a quiet whisper? I know that I am waiting for lightning as You quietly whisper my name. "Don't be

anxious about anything, but in everything, by prayer and
petition with thanksgiving make your requests to God and
the peace of God, which transcends all understanding
will guard your hearts and minds." (Phil. 4:6-7)

Yesterday, Masato went to church all by himself. Lord, you are in His life forever now. Please keep him close to your heart. I read a quote in a magazine by Paul Shane Spear that said, "You can't change the world, but you can change the world for one person." Lord, my world has been changed, and so, I believe, has Masato's.

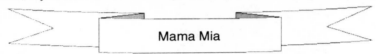

Mama Mia

God knows just what His daughter needs. My mom and grandmother (Nonna) came over to visit and we took a trip to Italy—"It-lee," according to my Nonna. We went to Venice, to the Leaning Tower of Pisa, and finally to Naples, which is where Nonna's family comes from. We had been warned that the further south you go in Italy, the more dangerous it is as far as being robbed. So, when we got off the train in Naples we had our guard up and eyes in the back of our heads. We got into a cab and asked the man to take us to our hotel. He rambled on and on in Italian, but then, to his surprise, my Nonna in a perfect Napolitano accent talked back to him. Well, that was all it took, and now this man became our best friend, taking us all over the city for free. He even knew where to find people who knew her parents and grandparents. For those of us who can trace our lineage directly to another country, it feels like a piece of you is put in place once you actually get to see your homeland. The two highlights were visiting Pompeii and being with Nonna when we went to Caivano, her mother's hometown. As a little girl, she was told stories about Mt. Vesuvius and Pompeii. It really was lifelong dream come true for her. The isle of Capri is beautiful, and I would love to come here with my husband if I ever get married.

When my mom and my nonna left, I knew the trip was one that will forever be in my memory. Three generations traveling together, and at seventy-four years old, boy can my nonna walk! She had had all those little Italian men eating out of the palm of her hand.

Not only was it fabulous to have my mom and nonna with me in our motherland, but I got to share my struggles and pray with them. The weight of my decision seemed to get heavier. I sensed that Bangkok was the place for me, even though I would be starting from scratch. But in Manila, things were already going on. There was a support team of leaders in place and the pastor who had been running the youth group was ready to hand it off to someone.

May 23, 1997

God opens doors and closes others. They think they have found someone to fill Bangkok, so Manila is now their first choice for me. I feel like Charlie Pridmore, the pastor of Union Church of Manila, and I have really clicked. They are looking at hiring me as the youth director and having an intern from California. That would answer my prayer of not being a loner in ministry anymore.

May 24, 1997

Lately I have felt a sense of urgency to share with these kids the truth of Jesus Christ. They deserve the truth—not sugar-coated so that they can make a choice. I need to stop protecting them, as I think they need it.

Yesterday, as a going-away present, I gave Tina Riedel
a "Pass it on" with Philippians 4:13 on it: "I can do
everything through him who gives me strength." She
carried it around with her all day. These kids are dying
to hear the truth. Who will bring my light to them?
Father, give me Your strength, courage, and boldness,
in love to share the truth wherever I go. For salvation
only comes through you.

It has been a difficult weekend. A fourteen-year-old Yugoslavian girl has nowhere to go and no one to turn to. Her father pushes her to become a professional tennis player, and that is why he brought her here from Yugoslavia. Yet he abuses and beats her up emotionally and at times physically threatens her. Lord, how I want her to know what a loving father is like! How I long for her to feel Your healing touch. Today I gave her a bible, but only the Holy Spirit can urge her to read it and transform her heart. Lord, give me wisdom in dealing with the father and brothers. One brother is in Cyprus, and the other is based in Atlanta but travels the world. They have lived through the abuse of the father and understand what Milana is going through. They also have the power to remove her from her father. Be with her father, Lord, and extend a portion of your amazing grace to him.

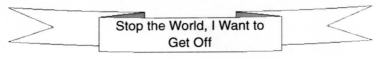

Stop the World, I Want to
Get Off

June 8, 1997

Here I sit on the train bound for Thalwil after a short
trip to Manila, Philippines. As I return, I am confused by
my emotions. I felt very at home there, and the people are
lovely. But I am very anxious about the job and whether I
am capable or not. There is a great deal of expectations

for the youth group. I like Charlie, the pastor, and his wife Darlene is a hoot.

Manila is much more westernized than I had imagined. Every fast-food joint is there, they all speak English, tons of movies, and it was cleaner than I was expecting, but traffic was worse. Lord, I give you the next few years of my life in Manila to melt, mold, fill, and use me. And if you would, please bring someone special into my life.

June 14, 1997

When it rains, it pours. It was a good weekend of golfing, but I returned home only to face a notice on my door of one unpaid 40-franc (approx. $30) fine from January for which I was to serve a one-day jail sentence because I didn't pay it. I went to the bank to transfer the Young Life money to the IPC and found that while I was in Manila, $3,500 had been withdrawn. I also got a call from a very upset mother who said that fifteen middle school kids have been waiting at Belleview train station for the scavenger hunt, and it was supposed to be her son's birthday party. This is one of those times where you want to yell, "Stop the world, I want to get off!" Sometimes I wish I was still a little girl with no responsibilities.

I have less than one week left in Switzerland, and I am getting anxious. After yesterday, I am so ready to leave, but what lies ahead means being very responsible. I feel like I have not been focused on Christ these last couple of weeks and it's been all Angie. Lord, I am feeling

*broken, weak, and alone—may I learn to let go of the raft
and drown in the ocean of your love. Lord, thank you for
your unfailing, never-ceasing unconditional love.*

You can only stay on the mountain so long. It's where you are refreshed and it's a time to rest, but most growth happens in the desert—or in my case, the islands. God is ready to stretch me once again; I hope I'm ready. Manila, Philippines, here I come! As I attempt to go through the departure gate in Zurich, I am abruptly reminded of that unpaid forty-franc fine and am detained and threatened with jail time unless it is paid. One last example of Swiss efficiency—that they could catch me leaving the country, so I gladly departed with my last forty francs and said *auf wiedersehen!*

Thrilla in Manila

Wow is it hot here! I was told that my air conditioning would be on 24/7 and I'm not even sure that will be enough. Maybe I will drop a few pounds, sweating so much! It's amazing how quickly the summer has passed, and I have just finished my first week in the Philippines. I have felt very welcome here by the Union Church of Manila. I live with the pastor of the church and his wife, Charlie and Darlene. They are a lot of fun and have three monkeys as pets. Every night after dinner, when we sit down to watch TV, they bring the monkeys in to watch TV with us. They also have a driver, a cook, and a few maids. This sort of life is so foreign to me, but it is expected of all foreigners to support the local economy and have maids, drivers, and cooks. However, being the independent, somewhat stubborn woman that I am, I decided I can manage on my own.

Aug. 11, 1997

> *Father, I thank You for all that You have done in my life. The times You've challenged me and wrapped Your arms around me. I want so much to abandon all of me to You. I thank You for loving this ragamuffin. You are the awesome Creator, and I marvel at Your wonders. May I never take it for granted again. Father, open my eyes to this new culture, that I may learn from them more about who You are.*

I am very excited about coaching at the International School of Manila. It took only ten days, but I was hired as the assistant varsity volleyball coach and as a substitute teacher. Praise God, as this will be my "in" to meet new kids. I also found a group of men who play basketball once a week at the high school, and they asked me to join them. This will be a great place for me. Being sports-minded does have its advantages when wanting to work at a school.

Did I mention how bad traffic was here? The church has given me a blue Tamaraw FX, which looks like jeep but is commonly used in the Philippines as a taxi. I start to feel comfortable driving from the Pridmores' home to the school, church, and back. It was August 20 and my first night joining the fellas for hoops at the high school. After our game was over, I hopped in my Tamaraw and headed down Makati Avenue. Traffic was really backed up. There were three lanes of traffic going each way, and we were bumper to bumper, moving about a foot a minute. Sometimes when it rains hard, the roads flood and it's a mess. What should take twenty minutes has been known to take eight hours! I guess it was one of those nights.

As I approached a major intersection just two blocks from the school, I saw traffic officers running the stoplight. This appeared to be part of the problem. When I got to the front of the line, just about to pass through the intersection, the officer motioned for me to stop and waved the cars traveling the other direction on. The officer then walked over to my window and asked me for my papers. Now, I had been warned that the police often ask for bribes, and I was determined not to give in. I guess I stood out in a crowd—a foreign woman behind the wheel was unheard of. I pulled out my license and proof of ownership. He took my papers and walked over to the other officers. After a couple of minutes (mind you, I was still in the middle lane of bumper-to-bumper traffic), more officers arrived on the scene. When the officer finally came back to me, I asked him what was wrong, and he proceeded to tell me that I was driving the wrong way on one-way street. *What?* "How can I be going the wrong way down a one-way street when all these other people around me are going the same way?"

He replied, "Ma'am, you are going the wrong way on a one-way street."

It was at this point that I was expecting him to ask for a bribe. But I was wrong. He said that the consequence of such an offense is six months in jail! He informed me that I would have to go to jail, and in order to get my car there, he would ride with me as an escort. I started getting very scared. The other officers had surrounded the car, and a motorcycle officer was now in front to escort me as well. I asked if I could make a phone call and they said yes, but I had no phone. I told them that I worked at the International School where the former president of the Philippines Fidel Ramos's wife works, and I could use their phone. They laughed and told me to ask her for driving lessons.

So this man got in the passenger side of the Tamaraw, with the motorcycle cop in front and now a police car behind. You would have thought I was a dignitary by the escort I was receiving. By now I was really very scared. The officer next to me was now trying to assure me that he would talk to the warden and ask her to let me off the hook. He also tried to convert me to his religion, a well-known cult in the Philippines called Iglesia ni Cristo. Neither provided much comfort to me. When we arrived at the Makati jail, all eyes were on me—the foreign woman. I was taken into the reception area, where they began to ask me all sorts of questions. As if it wasn't hot enough, I really started sweating now. The smell was so rancid that I thought I was going to throw up. *Oh, God, I need your help!* No one would know where I was. The only people who would have a clue, the Pridmores, thought I was at school playing, basketball. They would never know where to look for me. As the warden of the jail questioned me, I felt like I was the evening's entertainment. After four hours of interrogation, I asked if I could call the Union Church of Manila. When she asked why and I informed them that I also worked there, her tone changed. I don't know why I didn't think of it earlier, but the Philippines in general is a very Catholic and God-fearing nation. This woman looked around the room and said that I was free to go.

I got out of there quickly, jumped in my Tamaraw, and started to bawl as I drove off. When I got back to the Pridmores' and told them what had happened, Charlie got on the phone with the US Embassy to report the incident. It was then that I learned that this exact thing had happened to other American women and they were raped in jail. I started to cry again as I realized that this time openly confessing my belief in God saved me from great horrors. Thank You, Lord! I know there were people back home praying for my safety on that day.

Aug. 25, 1997

"Live lives worthy of God, who calls you into His kingdom and glory" (1 Thess. 2:9). Lord, what must I do to live a life worthy of You? I feel You working on my heart these days—challenging my heart. I can play the part of a Christian leader, but I have not yet learned how to descend with my mind into my heart and there stand before the Lord fully exposed, allowing all of His glory to penetrate my very being.

I can see how God has once again shown me that He is in control. My financial fears of leaving the security of teaching have been alleviated. God has provided my needs financially through the church and support back home, socially with other young single leaders. He's opened the doors at school for coaching and substitute teaching.

A wonderful revolution came to me the other day as I was thinking about Bigkis, the local Filipino Young Life ministry. I can't wait to get to heaven and meet Christians from all over the world. What a wonderful, glorious day that will be! The realization of the gospel reaching the world finally hit me.

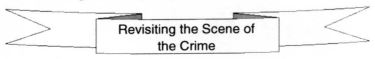
Revisiting the Scene of the Crime

Ironically, one of the long-standing ministries of the youth group I inherited was to go to the Makati jail once a month and visit the inmates. I guess they would have found me eventually! My eyes were opened to how horrific life was there. We brought them things they had requested the month before, like soap, toothpaste, paper, and pens. Then we sang songs with them and talked a bit. First we went to the men and then to the women. The men were piled high, with far more inmates per cell than beds. Most slept on a piece of cardboard on the floor. The women all seemed to have their own beds and more room.

The smell of body odor and fish (the latter being a Filipino staple) was so strong that many of the kids had to leave before they got sick. As I sat there trying to wrap my brain around this whole concept, I noticed a banner hanging above some of the inmates. It said, "When you visit the least of them in prison, you visited me." That is why we will continue to visit month after month. When the evening was done, we headed back to the church to eat ice cream and debrief.

Sept. 2, 1997

> *These twelve-hour days are hard. I need to make time for God, exercise and sleep. There is so much going on, getting ready for our first youth retreat to Calayra. I am lying here trying to survive after food poisoning that I got on the golf course. I will never be able to eat a tuna sandwich again.*

> *It will be a good thing when I move into my own place, so I can dictate my evening schedule more. As I write today, my heart is filled with joy—the joy of the Lord is my strength.*

We have started our "club" meetings with the high school, and it is going better than I expected. It is great to have a team—and what a team it is! We have two ladies who teach at another international school, Jim Charmley who is here with Bigkis, the ministry to the

Filipinos, Charlie, Darlene, and me. Each week so far, we have had new kids show up. Somehow we need to figure out a way to welcome them without embarrassing them. Lord, give me the wisdom and vision to best develop this group. How can we bring in more kids to hear and experience Your love? The group is a mix between kids from the International School of Manila and Faith Academy, where their parents are all missionaries in Southeast Asia. It makes for a very interesting discussion.

Sept. 8, 1997

> *Feelings are such a powerful thing. I realized last night that I don't express my own. I can feel deeply for someone else but can't articulate it. Last night, I just wanted to cry on one of my leaders' shoulders but I wouldn't allow myself that freedom. Why can't I show my feelings? I lie to myself and others when I do this. O Lord, when I prayed for You to search me and know me—see if there is any offensive way in me and lead me in the way everlasting, I didn't know that it was my inner being that is being held captive, not allowing Your amazing grace to heal me. This process of learning or allowing my innermost being to be fully Yours means I have to give up control. I can give up material things, family nearby, friends, but giving up control of my heart . . . Wow, why haven't I realized that I was controlling this too? Lord, give me strength to become weak so that Your amazing grace can make me strong.*

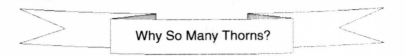

Why So Many Thorns?

I am encouraged by the many thorns in my flesh. First, there was the arrest for driving the wrong way down a one-way street (even though everyone else was going the same way), then food poisoning, and then the church van was stolen while we were at McDonald's. And now, an amoeba in my intestine and a bad back which means I am stuck on the toilet and it hurts too much to get off. I once again threw out my back. Only this time, I found out that I have two herniated discs in my lower back. My spirits are still okay as I try not to think of the future implications and restrictions. But this injury has made me homesick. Lucas called today, and it is so great to talk with him. What an awesome young man God is molding him into! I am very proud to have him as a brother.

This past weekend, our high school retreat at Caliraya, a beautiful resort a few hours out of town, was filled with wonderful moments. Some kids thought for the first time about who God is; some even began to have a relationship with Christ. Still others continue to ask questions and figure out exactly what they believe. Lord, I pray that they would continue to search for the truth. It's time to begin a more in-depth Bible study with many of them. Lord, give me wisdom on the logistics and strength and boldness when I invite kids. This is such an exciting time for many of them. Holy Spirit, I pray that You will break down the protective walls around their hearts and Your amazing love and grace would surround them.

Grace is such a wonderful gift. Father, I pray that I would become more gracious toward others. As things have slowed down, and as I have been bedridden, the awesomeness and unworthiness of the task before me seems overwhelming. I have no real training. I have been given many gifts, Lord, one of which is the ability to build relationships with kids. If I can do nothing else but love these kids unconditionally, that is what I will do. Anything, Lord, that You wish for me to do, it must come from Your hands, not mine.

As I read and study the apostle Paul's life, I realize how God used him—an untrained pastor to reach the world. For Paul's new vocation and vision was to spread the good news that we are reconciled to God by faith in Jesus Christ. A common verse that I have read hundreds of times has come to have new meaning these last couple of days: "I have been crucified with Christ and now longer live. The life I live in the body I live by faith in the Son of God who loved me and gave himself for me" (2 Corinthians 5:17).

It is the middle of October, and I have finally moved into my own house. It is a very large place, just a few blocks from the school and walking distance to the church. I decided to share a place with our new associate pastor, who has just arrived. I hope this helps to stave off the loneliness. I will miss living with the Pridmores and all the activity that goes on at their house.

Oct. 14, 1997

Today two bombs went off in downtown Makati, where I walk every day. One member of our church was injured. Every store is guarded by men with machine guns. I've never experienced such a lawless place.

Yvonne has been a gift from heaven. We hang out most nights and go to dinner. She is from Australia, around my age, single, and a Christian. She arrived a few weeks before I did, and many people at the church thought that she was the new youth pastor. Our favorite thing is to go to Starbucks around 11 at night. This is the

place to see and be seen here. This country has the rich
and the poor, no middle class.

As I entered Starbucks for the first time since moving into my own house, an aroma of familiarity filled me, and I felt like the Philippines was now home. I had weathered the storm and was now acclimated to my new environment. I had to learn the ropes the hard way in some instances, but now things were going to look up. And I'll take a tall skinny hazelnut latte with that, thank you!

CHAPTER 9

You Know When People Are Praying for You

If there was ever a season in my life when I needed protection, this was it. The ministry with kids was going very well. Both the middle school and high school groups were growing, and I had great leadership teams for both groups. This season of my life was much more about what God wanted to do in my heart than what He would do through me. We are often asked by missionaries to pray for them while they are in the field. Thank you to all of you who prayed for my protection, because I had no idea what I was in for.

As a trained educator who works with teenagers, I always knew that when faced with danger, I would sacrifice my own well-being for that of the kids. This protective mother hen was about to be put to the test! The middle school youth group night always started at McDonald's, which was two blocks away from the church we used. We would meet there, eat, and then walk back together. On this day, as we left McDonald's and attempted to cross the street—umbrellas in hand, since it had stopped raining—the traffic was horrible. We stood at the corner for several minutes, getting splashed by the cars zooming by. No one stops for pedestrians here. Finally there was an opening in the traffic, so we made our move and started to cross. Jim Charmley and Jenny Pool, two of the leaders, were up ahead of us.

Jamison Dion, an eighth grader, and I were behind them, and three eighth-grade girls behind us.

Just then, a woman driving a new Honda CRV pulled out and just missed Jamison. As we got to the other side of the street, she made a right turn and pulled up next to us. I stepped between her and Jamison so she would yell at me and not him. As she rolled down her window, I moved toward her to see what the problem was. As I approached her car, she reached into her glove compartment and pulled a gun on us. This is where the heroic Angie should jump in! But no, I freaked out and tried to hide behind a thin pole that covered about a quarter of my body. I yelled at the kids, "Save yourselves!" The girls started screaming, and the two leaders up ahead turned back. She wanted to know who hit her car. Apparently, when she drove past us, the tip of the umbrella that this boy was carrying hit her tire. I don't remember what I said, but she drove off and pulled up to Jenny and pointed the gun at her.

Jim mentioned later that he thought it was either a flare gun or a sawed-off shotgun. That's when my smarts really kicked in. I told two boys to run after her and get her license plate number! *Great idea, Feather, send them after a crazy woman with a gun.* So much for being the hero! Thank You, Lord, for hearing the prayers of other people. Thank goodness she did not turn back around, and we never saw her again.

Mar. 8, 1998

> *It's a sunny Sunday afternoon, and I am sitting at the pool, relaxing. If you can step back and enjoy the simple things in Manila, you can find an oasis. Lately I have begun to feel the uncertainty of the future. Why do I focus so much on the future, instead of the here and now? I still*

have over a year left here. My thoughts go from teaching to Young Life. Lord, where can I be the most useful to You? Or do I choose where to go and allow myself to be used wherever I am? I am twenty-seven years old now and am beginning to see the effects of age. I am also going through the stage where I am ready to settle down and think about raising a family. I know that there is much to learn about loving, patience, and commitment, but Lord, I am willing to invest the energy.

I continually think of Justin and his frustrations. Over Christmas, it was great spending time with my family, yet seeing Justin struggle was very hard. This was the first time I have been around him while he has had multiple seizures. But he is happy and in love. Lucas seems great and is growing up. Mom and Dad's marriage seems to be strengthening as the years go by.

Mar. 30, 1998

This past weekend was spent relaxing on a beautiful white beach in Boracay, Philippines. I forget how much I enjoy traveling and meeting new people. I must keep people as my priority, not places or activities. As each day passes here, I am learning more and more the value of being committed to people and relationships—looking to others' needs. Yet my needs and desires still are the overriding focus.

One day, I was on my way to one of the city's largest malls, known as the Mega Mall. I drove along EDSA, one of the main streets, and took the Mega Mall exit. A cop on a motorcycle came directly at me, so I changed lanes so I wouldn't hit him. He then made a U-turn and flagged me down. The violation? Swerving. Unbelievable, because if I hadn't, he'd be dead. He took my license and told me I could pick it up at the Quezon City police station. After a few minutes of being angry, I drove off. He then waved his arms at me, so I stopped. He drove up and said that I had forgotten my ticket. I then asked for his name and told him that I would tell my friends at Makati Jail about this. He then looked at my Union Church card, compared it to my license, and said, "I forgive you," and gave me back my license. In the meantime, I had taken all the money out of my wallet, so when he asked for a bribe—or "Christmas present" as they called it—I could show him that my wallet was empty. He let me go with a warning. Thank You, Lord, for hearing the prayers of other people.

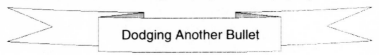

Dodging Another Bullet

It was Easter week, and I was house-sitting for the Merrifields, a beautiful American couple with a great house and even greater hearts. I looked forward to time away from my roommate, who was turning out to be awful to live with. One morning, I headed out the back door to take on my morning gardening duties. The house was surrounded and fortified by a large, high brick wall, so there was a great deal of privacy. I was dressed in my small pajamas with no shoes on. It took only two steps forward to realize that the door had locked behind me. I went around and checked all of the windows and doors, but nothing was open. A bit of panic started to set in. I looked outside the front gate for the neighbors' security guard, hoping that he could help somehow. He wasn't there. I couldn't leave the house dressed like I was. I had the landlady's phone number, my car keys, and shoes and clothes, but all were inside. Then I remembered Blythe Merrifield telling their maid to open a kitchen window for ventilation instead of the door. All of the other windows had bars, but this particular window had a screen. I found a small piece of wire, which I used to unscrew the corner screws. This took about fifteen minutes. I reached under the screen and prayed that the window was unlocked—it was. I pushed the window open and felt a huge wave of relief come over me. But then as I tried to stretch through the bars, under the screen, and around the window to the door, I found I was too short. Some supernatural thing happened to my arm and it stretched and stretched, but I could not reach the lock. I could, however, put my fingertips on the doorknob and use all the strength in my fingertips, and—*voila!*—the door opened. As soon as the door opened, it started to pour down rain.

Five minutes after that, the phone rang, and it was Blythe Merrifield. She had had a dream that someone had broken into the house but then concluded that, "I don't know what I am worried about. That place is built like Fort Knox and no one could break in." I assured her all was fine. Thank You, Lord, for hearing the prayers of other people.

I came to learn that Easter week is very holy, revered, and acknowledged in the Philippines. From Good Friday to Easter Sunday, the entire country shuts down—all TV, radio, restaurants, grocery stores, and malls shut down. I was not warned about this, because most foreigners go on vacation during this time. So in order to make the most of my time, I found a friend in the church and went for a hike to Lake Taol, which is in the center of an inactive volcano. It was a nice day and not overbearingly hot. We drove to our location, the only ones on the road. The rest of the country was honoring Jesus's death so no one was doing anything, including hiking.

We started to hike up a trail near the volcano. It wasn't too difficult of a hike but a nice excursion. We were very disappointed when we got to the lake to see that it had turned into a trash heap.

We had planned on spending most of the day at the lake but quickly decided to head back down the volcano. We were near the bottom where the path began to level off, when we heard three loud bangs and saw the sand just below our feet shoot up. We froze! Was someone shooting at us? Two more shots, and we ran as fast as we could to our car. We never saw where the shots came from, but we knew that was our sign to leave. Thank You, Lord, for hearing the prayers of other people.

Apr. 14, 1998

The end of the school year is just around the corner. Have I accomplished what I wanted to? I have many young acquaintances. It's time to get a bit deeper with these kids. I am really enjoying the Bible study at International School.

The middle school group has really turned into a joy. But it seems like typical me—after one year I begin thinking about moving on. What am I searching for in my restlessness? I have many wonderful friends and family around the world, yet I let my desire to be married dominate my relational energies. Lord, I want so badly to be content as a single person, yet my greatest fear is just that!

I had a great conversation with Justin today. We talked about his great worth in Christ. We spend an hour discussing the brain tumor seminar he went to, his new love Maria, and life in general. It was one of the best conversations we have ever had as adults. I sense that the Lord is stirring his heart once again

Apr. 14, 1998 continued

> *It's only been about eight hours since my last entry,*
> *and somehow this has become one of the worst days here.*
> *I don't know why my spirits are so low. I have no one*
> *here to turn to either. It seems like everyone at church is*
> *on my back. How can I please everyone? My computer*
> *is down, and it makes it impossible to do any work or*
> *send e-mails. My phone has been disconnected. I miss*
> *my family like crazy. But the worst thing is that there is*
> *no one here I can call or cry on their shoulder. Maybe I*
> *could call Blythe or Yvonne.*

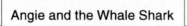

Angie and the Whale Shark

Sorsagon, Philippines, is on the southern tip of Mindanao—the largest island in the Philippines. It hosts the world's most perfect volcano, Mount Mayon. I joined Pastor Charlie, Darlene, and their son Jason on a family vacation. The purpose of our vacation was to swim with whale sharks. The World Wildlife Federation (WWF) was trying to teach the Filipinos that they can make more money by increasing tourism to see the whale sharks than by killing them and selling them to the Japanese. Now, let me tell you about whale sharks. These creatures are up to fifty feet long and swim in the murky water, where they suck up plankton in the ocean. Our assignment was to find a shark, jump in the water with our snorkeling gear on, and look for certain distinguishable characteristics so they could track these sharks. We were not supposed to touch them, and if they swallowed us—not to fear—they would spit us out. I personally think that was what swallowed Jonah! They told us we had to actually fear the tail more than the mouth, and if the sharks were spooked, they would dive down, where their tail could send us sailing. Understand that the movie *Jaws* ruined me for any future scuba diving, because I am deathly afraid of sharks and big fish.

Yet here I was, asked to go in the water in the ocean and swim with the largest fish in the sea. This was the most exhilarating and adrenaline-producing thing I have ever done. I, Angie Feather, actually swam in the open water with a fifty-foot shark. And, as one of my flippers fell off my foot and headed to the open mouth that was approximately eight feet wide and three feet high, I had to decide to lose the flipper or dive down and get it. I saved the flipper. I don't know what came over me, but never again would I have the strength to get in the water with a shark. Did I figure that since I was with the pastor, nothing would happen to me? Oh, and did I mention that I wore a bright red swimming suit and I am sure it looked like blood! Our trip was successful, as we found and swam with twenty-two different whale sharks. I was very exhilarated by this experience, but I will never again do such a thing. I only could muster up that kind of courage once.

Jun. 12, 1998

> *The mad exodus out of the Philippines is over for the summer. It seems an even greater number of people are moving than did from Zurich or Sophia. It's been a very low-key week but I have been able to spend some time with the kids. Plus I have been doing a lot of thinking. It seems I always start worrying about my future a year before I need to. What do I want to do next? What does God want me to do? I sense there will be some major decisions to be made this next school year. Part of me, a big part of me, wants to move back to the US, get a job teaching at a public school, and stay there awhile. I really miss teaching. Where this is, I don't know.*

I am really looking forward to my trip to China with Yvonne. She has become such a good friend to me; even though we have very different interests, we both love traveling to new places.

To start the summer off right, Yvonne and I decided to take a trip to China. It was incredible, climbing the Great Wall! We went to a more remote part of the wall, rented a couple of donkeys, and rode along the wall. Growing up, I viewed the Great Wall as an untouchable place. It was part of a communist country, and no one goes there. But now, to stand on this wonder of the modern world and look out just took my breath away. There was so much to see and experience there. I have been a lot of places in this world, but this place felt the most "foreign" to me. We even had the locals walking by and pointing at us, calling us "big nose." I guess our big western noses are a bit of an object of envy for them. Go figure!

After the trip, it was time to go home for a few weeks to see the family and eat peanut butter again.

Aug. 10, 1998

It is refreshing to be with my family again. As I get older, it is interesting to see the dynamics of our family change. Lucas is doing great. It amazes me, the influence I as an older sister have had on his life. Mom and Dad are good. I am enjoying them as friends and confidants more. Nonna is Nonna—full of life and baking pies. But I worry about Justin. His attitude toward life has turned sour. He is very negative, especially toward Mom and Dad. I wonder if the anger of getting cancer is finally surfacing. I know that being away from Maria while she is back in Spain is hard. He loves her so much. What would it be like to be in his shoes? Where has his faith in God gone? How can I help him see that his bitterness has changed his life?

San Diego was great. Visiting old friends is always fun. Perhaps I will move here when I am done in Manila. A stark realization hit me when I was walking down the street: If I move back to the US and teach, my entire lifestyle will change. No longer will I be able to spend freely or have friends who can do the same. I can't just pop over to another country for the weekend. I will be a poor schoolteacher on a budget, with friends who will be the same. That will be more of a culture shock than anything. As much as I don't want to be materialistic, this is a huge issue.

My Fuller Seminary class was great this summer. The professor, Chap Clark, really challenged my beliefs. What I believed to be true about God was shaken and asked to change. I must read and re-read Romans. Why would God create people that He wouldn't elect? He places the knowledge of Himself in everyone, and we are responsible to respond? I agree, but if God elects those who will go to heaven, then is it really free will or choice? And why create someone you don't elect? I still haven't wrapped my mind around this? I must study this more. Maybe I do not understand Him correctly. The God I serve chose me before the beginning of time to be made in His image.

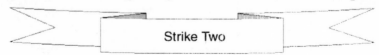

Strike Two

Upon my return to the Philippines, I wanted to re-integrate gradually back into the culture, so I went to TGI Friday's for my first meal. Unfortunately, my purse was snatched right out from under me. It was found at 4:00 a.m. in the men's restroom. What a frustration it was to lose my keys, credit cards, and address book. Then, to top it all off, the next day I drove the one mile from my house back to TGI Friday's to pick up what was left of my purse, and a monsoon rain started. It ended up taking me four hours to drive the mile back to my house, because of the flooding and traffic in the streets. Why did I even go back? Maybe I should have stayed back in the States to spend more time with Justin. Was I being selfish?

Thankfully, my work with the kids was going well, but the Pridmores were now thinking about moving on to another country. They had been such a resource for me that I really didn't want to be without them. My walk with God was really struggling as well. It seemed that all of my time was spent studying, in preparation to teach, and not doing anything for my personal growth. I was not spending time with God anymore. Do other church leaders struggle with this? How can I be in the Word so much, yet feel so devoid of it?

Nov. 26, 1998

> *Lord, I pray that You would help me through this. Continue to work on my heart, and Lord, please give me direction. Lord, please, make Your will known to me.*

> *Lord, I want so badly to share my life with a man. To share my hurts, my joys, my dreams, my gifts. To grow old with. I want a loving father to my children. Someone who will teach them how to love You and love life. Lord, You know my heart's desire. May I never stray from You. I have strayed so far; Lord forgive me.*

Our middle school group had a monthly mission to an orphanage and birthing home. Darren and Deborah Gustafson, who were the key volunteers for this group, ran the orphanage. So we took our middle school kids there every month, just to play with the orphans. It was one of the highlights of each month. There were a few of those kids that I would love to adopt and make my own. Unfortunately, if you live in the Philippines as a foreigner, you cannot adopt, to prevent people from just using them as servants and not children. Perhaps when I return to the United States, I will one day adopt from here.

Another bright spot each night was when I drove home from work down Makati Avenue. Cherry Pie and her other friends would see my car, and all would come running and jump on my car. They would yell, "Angie, Angie, Angie!" as they ran. I developed an amazing relationship with these street kids. They even hung on as I drove down the street very slowly. I made sure to have my leftovers or food in my car for them. One day, Cherry Pie showed up with a new haircut and a perm! I guess no matter what your living situation is like, having beautiful hair is very important for a girl. I will have to remember this next time we take the middle school kids to visit with these street kids. We always brought KFC, and now we would remember to add perfumes and hair products.

As the end of my contract was in sight, I was once again uncertain where I wanted to go or what I wanted to do. I was beginning to feel homeless. The past week or two had been difficult. Kids here really struggled since Charlie and Darlene left for Venezuela. They had been such a stable force for the international community.

Feb. 14, 1999

> *I am really feeling an urge to get back into teaching,*
> *yet I do feel obligated to stay here at Union Church.*
> *Lord, I need You to take over my life right now. I am not*
> *thinking rationally and need You. If I leave here, where*
> *do I go? Lord, what is next for me? Do I push on with my*
> *master's in psychology? These feelings of being homeless*
> *and alone are so strong. Why do I go through these*
> *periods of such little faith? Lord, I long to be wrapped*
> *in Your arms of love!*

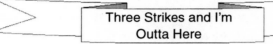

Three Strikes and I'm
Outta Here

From March 5-7, we had our second annual middle school retreat. All I can say is that I felt the Holy Spirit was there and totally working in the lives of the kids. Wayne Alguire was our speaker, and he was fantastic. He was really able to connect with these kids. He worked for Levi's, and it was the first time I had seen brand-new jeans with holes built in. The kids thought he was "the bomb" in those pants. After the first night of the retreat, we were very excited about how the kids were really engaged in all the activities and actively listening to the speaker. It was going to be a great weekend.

It seems that nothing ever goes as expected here. I was stung on my back by a bee my first day of the retreat, and unbeknownst to me, I have a pretty serious bee-sting allergy. I started to go into anaphylactic shock. My throat closed up, making it extremely hard to breathe, and my stomach cramped up, which caused me to throw up repeatedly. I thought I just had a bad cold and the flu. As we were on a small island in the middle of nowhere, there was no medical facility nearby. And it was only on my way home that I had made the connection with the bee sting. Looking back on previous stings, I had had an allergic reaction, but each time it got worse. The first time I noticed a reaction was when I stepped on a bee on the shore in Israel. I thought it was just a strange Israeli bee that caused my entire foot to swell. I now have to carry an EpiPen, in case I get stung again. Because of this, the other leaders had to really step up, and they did great.

The church asked me to stay on at least another year. At the time, I did not feel convicted to stay, but soon the urgency to leave Manila died down. I had agreed to entertain the idea of staying another year. Then, when I was crossing the street in downtown Makati, on my way to meet with church leaders at Starbucks, I was hit by a black BMW. I was wearing a dress and high heels, and in the middle of the day, as I used the crosswalk, I saw this BMW out of the corner of my eye. At the last second, I was able to push up from the front bumper so that when the car hit me, I ended up on the hood of the car instead of under the car. When the car stopped, I stared through the driver's window, but it was so darkly tinted, I could not see in. I sat there on the hood, waiting for the driver to get out and someone to help me. There was a large gathering of people, but no one offered a hand. After a few seconds, I got off the car and started to open the driver's door, but the car sped off. I stood there dumbfounded.

As foreigners, we had been told that there was a law that now made it illegal to run back over someone if you hit them. Prior to this, if someone was hit by a car, it was rumored that they would then back up over them to make sure they were dead, because otherwise they would have to pay for their hospital bills. This way, if they died, there was no financial responsibility. This was now illegal, which was a good thing for me so he didn't run me over again. In shock, I made my way to Starbucks, wondering when the next flight out of the country was leaving!

May 4, 1999

It's hard to believe that I am just about finished with my second year here in Manila. The church has moved into its temporary building while they tear down and build a new building. I am ready to leave here and find a more permanent home in the US. I am feeling more and more confident that counseling kids is what I want to do. The recent shootings at Columbine High School in Colorado have really helped me to realize that this is where my passion is right now. The past two weeks, teaching at the International School of Manila, has opened my eyes up once again to the hurting at a school.

As I sit outside Starbucks at the Rockwell Building, I watch a young couple and their baby. Lord, I long to love a man enough to want to have a baby with him. I desire the companionship and stability that comes with a family. I desire to walk closer with You, Lord. Working for a church has not helped my spiritual life. Now the "spiritual" is my job; before, it was my desire. Help me to get that desire back. I must begin my day with You, Lord. I cannot remember the last time I read the Bible without an ulterior motive. Lord, help me give my heart back to its true love so that the rest of my life would reflect that love.

Father, I also pray that You would be with Justin and Maria as they prepare to be united in marriage in two weeks, and Lucas and Stacy as their relationship deepens. Thank You for bringing two special women to my brothers, Lord. What is life all about if it's not about

*loving people? Lord, may I make people my focus and
think of the positive, instead of dwelling on the negative.
Life's too short and too exciting to not be lived to the
fullest.*

Habitat for Humanity was coming to the Philippines for the big International Jimmy Carter Project. Every other year, they pick an International location, with President Jimmy Carter as their spokesman, and this year, they chose two locations in the Philippines. They were going to build five hundred homes in one week. On the last day of the build, they solicited pastors from various churches to come build, and I was chosen from Unions Church. I love doing hands-on service, and I was very excited. We all met at one location, where we were bused down and they showed us the house we were to finish. It was great working side by side with other church pastors and knowing that some family would now have a place to live.

It was so hot and humid that I drank a bottle of water about every forty-five minutes. The event was very organized, with volunteers handing out water and oranges to help keep us hydrated. They also had an amazing system for feeding the thousands of volunteers in an orderly manner. When they came to our house and told us it was time for us to go to lunch, I was very ready for a break. I went through the food line, got my plate and two more bottles of water, and began to look for a place to sit. As I stood there looking for someone from my house, a Secret Service agent started yelling and waving at me and calling me Mary. I looked behind me and then around me and realized that he was yelling at me. So I walked over to him, and he asked me if I would sit at this table and save it for the president of the United States. I think he had me confused with one of the Habitat workers, but I quickly agreed.

So I sat down, exhausted, and slowly began to eat my meal. People would begin to sit at my table, and I would say, "I'm sorry, but this is saved for the president." Soon, a few other Americans sat down at my table, and it was clear that they were some of the president's inner circle. One guy even had a watch that would record the temperature three times a day, and they were discussing the temperatures throughout the week. I just sat there silently and listened. Then a woman came and sat next to me and pointed at one of my bottles of water and asked whose water it was. Without looking directly at her, but noticing that her hands suggested that she was an older woman, I offered her my water. As I turned to hand it to her, I noticed the name on her name tag—Rosalynn Carter. I was sitting next to the former first lady! Soon, former president Jimmy Carter came and sat at the head of the table. He joined in the conversation about the temperature. I just sat there. It was like I didn't exist. No one asked me who I was or why I was sitting with them. For a moment, I was part of the president's inner circle. Then, all of a sudden, a Secret Service agent came up told the president about table in the shade—and as quickly as they came, they left. What a great way to end my time in the Philippines.

CHAPTER 10

San Francisco Unified Is No Place for the Ruffled

For a time, I had been waiting for God to speak to me in a thunderstorm, typhoon, or jail cell, but instead it was a gentle whisper in my ear when He told me it was time to return to the United States. Justin's condition had worsened, and I needed to be able to get to him in a day. I also felt that God was leading me back into teaching and it was time to leave Young Life. So I landed a job teaching biology at the International Studies Academy, a public school in the San Francisco Unified School District. It was an inner-city public school on San Francisco's famous Potrero Hill, housing the Potrero Hill housing projects where OJ Simpson grew up. This was as far from the Private International Schools as you can get, even though it had a similarly fancy name. Instead of the big campus on lush acreage, it was a city block of all cement. My class size went from ten or fifteen to thirty-five or forty, and there was no air conditioning.

I chose San Francisco because I wanted to live in a diverse place, and San Francisco definitely fit that definition. I also wanted to try inner-city teaching. I found the perfect fit, school-wise. Unfortunately, because of high rent prices, I had to live across the Bay Bridge near Oakland on a small island called Alameda. This meant driving over the bridge every day, and my commute was about fifty minutes each way. I did find a way around the toll and a way to speed up the trip. I would swing by the bus stop in Alameda and pick up two strangers so I could drive through the carpool lane. How safe that was, I don't know. Once I even had a guy look in the car, and when he saw me driving, he said no thanks; he would rather take the bus!

My first day of work, I wanted to arrive at school extra early, to make sure I was all ready for the kids, and boy, was I nervous. I started up Potrero Hill, which is one of those famous hills in San Francisco that is very steep and goes on for blocks. As I neared the school, I saw five police cars surrounding the building. Nerves now turned to fear! Thankfully, it was just a practical joke; some kids had broken in and flooded the second floor of the school as a prank. Out of thirty-three teachers, fifteen of us were new that year. There was an extremely high turnover rate at our school. This was no place for the meek or nearly retired!

This was such an eye-opening experience for me, and I had never felt so needed and appreciated. It was like starting over as a first-year teacher. I had only been in small private schools where the kids did everything I told them to do. Now I had about thirty-five students per class, in an old elementary school building, and they were . . . let's say a *challenge*. The diversity was great, but the facility and resources were horrific. I quickly clung to my Italian heritage in order to fit in better with some sort of ethnicity and began to learn an entire new vocabulary, one of inner-city teenagers from California. I loved it. It challenged me in ways I had never been challenged, and I found my teaching skills improving in order to keep the students focused and entertained. I discovered a side of me that I had not known before, and I was thriving in this environment. I taught six biology classes each day and coached varsity volleyball. Life moved at an extremely fast pace.

Creativity came into play when I had to come up with ways to manage the behaviors in my class. I became known for two of my strategies: 1) If the students cursed around me, they had to drop and give me ten push-ups, even in the middle of class. (If someone swore, no matter where I was, and one of my students was nearby, they would say, "Oh, Ms. Feather, so-and-so needs to give you ten," to the point that eventually the entire school knew my expectations), and 2) If a boy was acting out, I challenged him to a football-throwing contest. Even if I didn't win—which I did 90 percent of the time—they were so impressed with my arm that they respected me and did not act out in class. Soon, my class became such a fun place to be, and the kids started to learn. In fact, some students liked my class so much that they flunked just so they could retake it the next year! Eventually, I knew every student in the school because I was the only biology teacher, and every student had to take biology in order to graduate. This also gave me some leverage with them.

But it wasn't all fun and games. There were heartaches and homelessness, teen pregnancies and helplessness like I had never experienced. God told me my role was to be an encourager—to be the students' biggest fan and to let them know that I believed in them. Throughout my six years there, we had two student shootings on campus, and one student was stabbed. Multiple times we had to lock down the school as we searched lockers and found guns.

Basketball was a constant source of adventure. Since our gym was not regulation size, our home games were played at the YMCA in the Tenderloin, a drug infested, crime ridden area of down town San Francisco. Very few people came to watch, but the first two rows were always packed with the homeless people who used that facility. Talk about intimidating the opponent! One day, on our way to a game, the girls had gone ahead of me on the bus as I took the managers in my car. I pulled up to the front of the school, and the girls loaded in. My car was pointed downhill, when suddenly, a motorcycle came up the hill on our side of the road. Next thing I knew, the motorcyclist hit us head-on, and on impact, flew over my car. The entire front end of my car was smashed in, but we were all okay. The motorcyclist was so wasted that he got up and stumbled down the hill away from the accident. Even though his bike was pinned under a van parked across the street, the police were never able to track him down.

Meanwhile, the girls at the gym were furious with me for not being there on time. When I told them we had to reschedule because I was a wreck at the moment, thinking this guy was dead, they protested. They were certain that the other team thought we were rescheduling the game as a sign of weakness. Nice to know they were so concerned about us! Another time, in the middle of the game, the police burst in and arrested several students in the crowd who were carrying guns.

Yet among these students there were many diamonds in the rough. I discovered in my biology and AP biology classes some very gifted minds. I saw so much potential in a few students, and I wanted so badly for them to see their potential as well. One teacher who believes in you can have a huge impact on your life—in fact, that is one major reason I decided to become a biology teacher to begin with. I always told my students that when they became a famous scientist and discovered the cure to a major disease, they needed to name it after me. They could name either the cure or disease, just as long as I got some credit for their success.

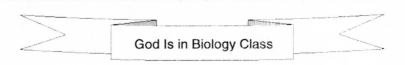

God Is in Biology Class

I started volunteering a little with Young Life Mission District. We took kids to Young Life's Woodleaf and Malibu, and it was great. One particular young man left his imprint on my heart and my faith. This young junior was in my biology class. His name was Bat, and he was from Mongolia. Bat did not speak much English, but like most students from other countries when they arrive here, he worked very hard in class and took full advantage of his new educational opportunities. Bat had to work longer and harder than anyone because of the language barrier. I found out that a simple homework assignment that should take about thirty minutes would take him two to three hours. He had a very positive disposition and loved school and basketball. I was helping to coach the varsity boys' basketball team at this point, and so I got to know Bat well.

The next year, Bat was in my AP biology class. I was worried that this would just be too overwhelming for him, as it was such a demanding class, even for native English speakers. One day after class, I was talking with him about his homework, and he shared with me how he stayed up all night, reading and doing his homework to the extent that he sometimes had to study in his bathroom. He lived in a loft with his father, and when his father drank too much, the only safe place was the bathroom, where he would lock himself in to study. It became clear during the course of the year that Bat had an amazing mind and needed to go to college. The problem was that he was here illegally. California is very friendly and fair to "undocumented" students, but Bat wanted to be here legally. A professor at San Francisco State had seen the quality of his lab work and was also trying to get him into school. He even arranged a meeting with a UC Berkeley professor for us.

It was the day before I was taking other students from our school to Young Life's Woodleaf Camp, and Bat and his father had offered to treat me to lunch, to show their appreciation for helping him. It was at lunch that I asked him what he was doing this next week, and when he said "nothing," I invited him to camp. He jumped at the opportunity, and I told him that he had to get $100 to the area director by 4 p.m. that day, in order to reserve a spot. Bat not only got the money, but on his way to deliver it, he was mugged and refused to give it up. He arrived at the Young Life area director's door beaten and bloody, but with his $100.

Bat heard about Jesus for the first time in his life, and at the end of the week asked Jesus into his heart as his Lord and Savior. Talk about a life-changing event! Then, as if that was not enough, his faith was instantly put on trial when he returned. He had applied for a visa because he wanted to be legal, and he had a court date to plead his case. Twice prior to this court date, the judge had denied him a visa, and now it was his last chance. He either got the visa or would be sent back to Mongolia. Part of the problem was when Bat arrived in this country, some lawyer made up a story about abuse in Mongolia, and Bat was not safe there. This was not true, but Bat signed the document because he did not speak English and had no idea what the lawyer wrote. When Bat took the stand that day, he clenched a small Bible in his hands and refused to tell a lie or embellish the truth. The judge even tried to give him a way out by asking Bat if he was sure there was no reason why he needed refugee status and was not safe in Mongolia. Bat refused to lie. Then the judge said, "Well, you leave me no choice. The law is very clear that you must fit into one of the five categories in order to be a legal refugee in this country. However, I am going to grant you a visa, because we need more men in this country who are honest and of your character." Praise God!

As much as I struggled as an AP biology teacher with the challenge of teaching evolution, in order for the kids to pass the final national exam, I found more opportunity to share Jesus and Creation than any other time during that course. I will always remember a young Chinese girl named Winnie, who also played on my volleyball team, asking, "Ms. Feather, what do you believe? Do you believe in evolution or Creation?" Talk about an open door to share my faith in class!

Casa Builders

I started to coach cross-country, and that opened the door for great conversations with kids. Just before our season was set to start, our athletic director came into my classroom to show me the results from the Bay to Breakers race that previous weekend. The Bay to Breakers is a famous race of about one hundred thousand people—mostly in costume, some in their birthday suits—that runs from the bay to the ocean, up and over the hills and through San Francisco. One of our students, Dawit, who was Ethiopian, finished this seven-mile race in the top one hundred! He proved to be just the lift our team needed and had great leadership qualities to match his athletic abilities. His dynamic personality drew more and more students to join the cross-country team, especially our international students.

Even though I was one of the slowest runners on my team, I ran with the students every day. This proved to be a great opportunity to really get to know these students. Without exception, they always asked me about my faith and belief in God. Most of them struggled with what they believed. We became such a close group that we even decided to go on a house-building project together. So we started raising money and gathering tool belts. With the approval of the school and school board, we joined with Casa Builders, a Christian organization that builds homes in Mexico. I had joined them a few times and had become very good friends with the Casa Builders. I thought this was the perfect opportunity to take these kids, who think they have nothing to offer anyone, into a situation where they have so much to offer. Moreover, they would be around Christians and hopefully see Christ in a new way.

It was a great trip, and almost everyone on the cross-country team joined us, as well as a few other students. We drove down from San Francisco in a caravan with other Casa Builders. For a few of the kids, this was their first time out of the Bay Area. We stayed at an orphanage, so when we weren't building, we were playing with the orphans. This had a greater impact on many of the kids than the building did.

When it was time to go home, we woke up early Sunday morning in order to get home before it was too dark. We anticipated a long wait at the Mexican-US border. The plan was, once one vehicle got across, it would pull off at the first exit and wait for the others. It was a good plan; we just overlooked a few details. When my van pulled up to the checkpoint, they asked for everyone's passport. In my van, we carried US, Ethiopian, Eritrean, El Salvadorian, and Chinese passports Unbeknownst to us, two of the students, one Ethiopian and one Eritrean, had refugee status in the United States and a one-time entry visa. This entry would make number two! They refused to let these two students back into the United States and insisted that they would have to go back to their home countries. This posed several problems, mostly because their families were all in San Francisco and because they were refugees who would not be allowed back in their home countries.

We put our heads together, and the other chaperone in my car took the rest of the students and the van into the United States to meet up with the rest of the group, to figure out what we could do. Meanwhile, the three of us grabbed our sleeping bags and backpacks, and with our heads hung low, walked back into Mexican territory to await our destiny. Luckily, if you're just near the border, certain cell phones work. The down side of the cell phones working is that by now, the principal called every thirty minutes to ask our status. The group decided that they would all drive back to San Francisco, but one woman, Karen, who had her car, would come back and stay with us until we got this settled. I was very thankful for her friendship, support, and car. Here I was, this great international traveler, and I never thought to check re-entry visas.

The four of us headed back to the orphanage, where the head of Casa Builders was, to stay the night. We had been informed that there was nothing we could do on a Sunday to try to correct the problem and that we needed to show up at 6:00 Monday morning to get in line. So that is what we did. I was very proud of the kids for being so brave. Unbeknownst to me, when we had them call home to explain the situation, they both made up a story that the border patrol only let US passport holders cross the border on weekends and the kids would have to wait until Monday to cross. They didn't want to scare their families. Of course, they said all this in their own languages, so I had no idea until later about what was said. We gathered around the dinner table that night and prayed and prayed for God to help us out. The kids fell asleep at 6:00 that night, exhausted from the stress. Karen and I could get into the United States with no problem, but these poor kids were looking at never going back to their homes or families.

"Come to me, all you who are weary and burdened, and I will give you rest. Take my yoke upon you and learn from me, for I am gentle and humble in heart, and you will find rest for your souls. For my yoke is easy and my burden is light." (Matthew 11:28)

The next morning, we were up early, and at the office they instructed us to go to the border by 5:45 so we could be first in line.

Finally, at 9:00 a.m. they let us in! We explained our situation, and they told us to wait. And wait we did. As we waited, we saw person after person in a similar situation approach this desk only to be told, "Too bad, you cannot reenter the United States." Most of these people were college students who had just gone to Mexico for the weekend. Thank the Lord that my two students were under eighteen, or there would have been no hope. Finally, at 5:00 p.m. that day, we received two one-time entry visas, each costing $500. We would have paid any amount for the visas, because they were priceless to us, but fortunately one of the other Casa Builders paid the bill for us. Karen took the car across the border and waited at McDonald's, while the three of us had to literally walk across the border. We actually held our breath until we crossed the border, and the moment we did, we started jumping up and down and hugging each other. When we met up with Karen, the four of us bowed our heads and thanked God for providing a way.

Needless to say, when we dropped those two kids off at about 2:00 the next morning, their parents couldn't stop hugging and thanking us for bringing them home safely. We all recognized the potential devastation we evaded and how God had answered our prayers. And only by the grace of God was I able to keep my job after that!

God worked through me, but once again, in my innermost being, I hurt. I was going through the motions, just trying to survive the moment. I knew that God used me in the lives of these kids and that all the adversity I underwent while living overseas had made me stronger. I knew I would not have survived my first two years in San Francisco without the hard times overseas. I just didn't realize that life can be just as hard in the United States as in a third world country. I was so exhausted each night when I got home, I did not read my Bible, pray, or journal. I was just surviving. Then I heard a gentle whisper: "Draw near to God and He will draw near to you" (James 4:8a).

CHAPTER 11

Good-bye, My Brother

I have lived all over the world, isolated from everyone and everything I knew, yet I had never felt more alone than I did living in Alameda, California. I continued to run, attend church, and work long hours. The busier I was, the less time I had to think. "The heart is deceitful above all things, and desperately wicked; who can know it?" (Jeremiah 17:9)

My family called in hospice to take care of Justin and help my parents, as Justin was now bedridden in their house. Hospice sent a nurse out every day to take care of his needs; they met with my parents and us to explain the dying process, so we knew what to expect. They made going through Justin's weakening state survivable, and my family will be forever grateful to hospice. It was so hard to see this once-strong, athletic man lying in a bed, unable to do anything for himself. He was confined to a medical bed in our parents' home so they could care for him and help his wife Maria during her pregnancy.

I went home in February for my thirtieth birthday and to see Justin. I was able to sit with him, hold his hand, and tell him how much I loved him. Some days, he had the sparkle in his eyes, and other days, his eyes were just glazed over. It was very difficult to see him in that condition, because he had always been so strong and full of life. I had not spoken to God in many months and could not gather any strength from Him. The tests showed that Justin had three new tumors in his brain. God had healed him completely thirteen years ago, but in the process, the radiation treatments that initially killed the large tumor had also caused three new tumors. Justin had lost his ability to speak, eat, walk, or even sit up. Once in a while, he could squeeze my hand. *This really can't be happening to us.*

Apr. 8, 2001

> *Oh Lord, my heart aches so badly. Justin is suffering so much. Lord, I can't stand the hurt and pain. Please, Lord, heal him. Little Anaya was born in March, and she needs a daddy to love her. Maria needs her husband. I need my brother. Lord, please bring Justin to a state of peace with You.*

> *Lord, I need You. I know these past four years I have tried to control my life. Look at what a mess it is. I am at the lowest I've been in a real long time—perhaps ever. My heart hurts so much. I want to be able to lean on You again. But I can't remember how. The pain hurts so much, I can't even pray, but Lord, hear the cries of my heart and soul—longing for Your arms to wrap around me.*

> *I long so much to be loved and to love with all my heart and strength in a mutual love. I watch the love between Maria and Justin, and I see how faithful two people can be to each other. I want to experience that kind of love. I know that Maria will never regret loving Justin.*

Lord, where should I be? Should I be in Colorado, near my family? Is this my selfishness wanting to be in a big city? Lord, take away the pain. Give me the strength to handle it. Give all of the family the strength to cope and peace of mind about letting Justin go and releasing him to You.

Justin's health got worse. I came home to meet his baby girl Anaya and watched the two of them take naps together. Justin was in his chair, and Anaya would be propped up on his chest; they slept so soundly together. I was still unable to pray—there was so much hurt inside of me. What happened to all those years overseas when I depended on God for everything?

On July 20, 2001, Justin went to be with the Lord. This was a letter I wrote in my journal on my plane ride home to be with the family and help plan his funeral:

Dear Justin,

As I think of you, so many songs run through my head, each one capturing a different time, event, or emotion in our lives. I can remember ever so slightly the really strong hugs and kisses you gave me as a toddler. Then, when we were in elementary school and middle school, one song sums it up: "Hit Me with Your Best Shot." You used to taunt me with that song, and the moment I would give in and let one fly, I would have to run for my life. You would chase me for hours, and whether you actually hit me or not, I don't know. But what I do remember is you sitting on my chest, either squashing my nose with your thumb or thumping relentlessly on my chest. And then, hours later, when Mom would show up, I would

142

start to cry so you would get in trouble—even though I started it.

But then we entered high school. You were the big senior on campus with all the friends. I was a lowly little freshman. I don't exactly know how it happened, but all of a sudden, instead of wanting to hurt me, you began protecting me—mostly from dating your friends. You became my advocate, supporter, and friend. I never realized how lucky I was at the time. I'll never ever forget the time you told me I could do anything. Wow!

As the years have passed and I have come to see you for the incredible man God created, the song "Hit Me with Your Best Shot" now has new meaning. Life has really hit you with its best shot, yet through it all, you continue to touch lives. You depict what life is all about—loving God and loving others. As I look at all the people that call or send letters and I hear their stories about how you touched their lives, I realize that you really understood what life is about—people. You are my hero! Sure, [when I was] a little girl, you would always speak for me. Whenever someone would ask a question, you would answer. But that's because you love people. I know that in 1986, when God performed a miracle on you—it was for a specific reason. He wanted to use you. And you allowed him to. Maria and baby Anaya are proof of that.

I am going to miss you so much. It breaks my heart that you won't ever have met my future husband or my kids. And that Anaya will not have you here physically.

"I have fought the good fight, I have finished the race, I have kept the faith. Now there is in store for me the crown of righteousness which the Lord, the righteous judge will award to me on the day—and only to me, but also for all who have longed for his appearing." (2 Timothy 4:7-8)

One very bright spot in this dark time was that my little brother Lucas and Stacy were married two weeks before Justin passed away. She is the perfect fit for him.

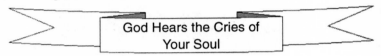

God Hears the Cries of Your Soul

Jan. 2, 2002

It's been a long time since my last entry. 2001 was a year of much pain and sadness. I didn't realize that depression had set in. I had been lonely and sad before but never depressed. On July 20, Justin went to be with Jesus. Only God knows the pain associated with the loss of a sibling.

As I read back through my journal, I realize that I will have many of the same struggles I had years ago. Lord, why do I bury my feelings so far down deep inside? I have allowed the world to control me instead of letting Jesus guide me.

I realize now that it is time to get healthy. I need a spiritual renewal. The last few years, I have only merely talked the talk. The pain of Justin's death numbed my spirit. SPIRIT, COME ALIVE! "I can do all things through Christ who strengthens me" (Philippians

4:13). I cannot be all things to all people—be true to yourself and who God created you to be. I think I need counseling to break this pattern of not allowing myself to feel. I realize that I keep people at a distance. What am I hiding? Am I afraid of the real me? Afraid I won't measure up to "their" expectations? I need to allow God to heal me. I know that the only way to truly appreciate things is to have felt the pain of loss and sorrow. I even thought I was in love once, but it wasn't a healthy love. No love excluding God can be good love. Lord, I know You will bring a love to me when "we" are both ready to be transparent and love.

Lord, I pray that I would become more transparent/ real/honest. I need a group of friends to help me and a church body in which to grow. Father, I thank You that You hear my prayers and You know my needs more than I do. I want to follow You. I want to allow You to live through me—fully and wholly without the worldly pressures overwhelming me. Lord, as this season of my life ends, I thank You for the pain and the desert. For I know that only through this can I truly appreciate the joys and mountaintops. Let my faith come alive. Let my energies go toward living for God, not for others. Lord, I have been so sinful. My life of confession has been nonexistent. I know that You will forgive all my transgressions. Lord, I thank You for those who have been praying for me. I have been spiritually numb, and it's time to wake up. Lord, the tears I shed are tears of joy that You are faithful and love me in spite of me. Tears of sadness that I could let You down so consistently and tears of hope for the future. Lord, I thank You for my

*sister Maria—for her friendship, for her love, and for her
spirit. Continue to draw her nearer to You.*

*Lord, take my heart, take my soul, Lord, I'm beggin'
You to take control. Of my body, of my mind, teach me
how to leave myself behind.*

God has proved in my life to use the most unlikely of situations
and people to work in my heart. God knew I needed to make some
changes. I knew I needed to make some changes, but I didn't know
how. Then, one day, I was walking to my car in the morning, just like
I did every morning. The man who lived across the path from me,
Stan, came up and said, "Do you know that there is a man that sits at
your bedroom window every morning?" WHAT?! You have got to be
kidding me. He went on to tell me that he saw this man sitting in the
bushes, looking in my window and occasionally looking across the
courtyard in the window of a young girl. He gave me a description
of the man, and I immediately called the police.

We decided set up a sting operation, where I would intentionally
leave my blinds cracked open a little bit and the man across the way
would get a better look at him and call the police. Well, this didn't
work, so we waited. There was a neighbor of mine that I would see
everywhere I went—the gym, grocery store, golf course. He lived
about two doors down, and I ran into him on our path. I shared with
him what was happening and described the man to him, but he had
not seen the voyeur either. Then the very next day, I was sitting in my
living room stretching after a long run and my curtains were open. A
few people passed by, and then my neighbor Stan, who had seen this
peeping tom, ran over and said the stalker had just walked by. The
only person I could remember seeing walk by was the nice man that
I saw everywhere I went, and he was carrying two Target bags.

My neighbor said, "He was carrying two Target bags!" I went stone cold. This man had been stalking me and was everywhere I had been. I called the cops, and they came over, went to the man's house, and talked to his wife because he was not home. I had no idea he was even married, because I never saw him with a woman. They then made a line-up of pictures to show the neighbors, and several identified him as the man who sat at my bedroom window. The next night, before the restraining order was issued, he knocked on my door. Had it been the previous night, I would have gladly invited him in, but tonight, with trembling hands and fear surging through my body, I called the police and locked myself in the bathroom.

Once the restraining order was given, I was allowed to get out of my lease and move, and this man was forced to move as well. This was just the move I needed. I found a great place across the bay in a town called Burlingame and in the process found a fabulous church. I was instantly plugged into a small group Bible study, made some great lifelong friends, and God started to work on my heart. I felt the weight of depression just fall off of me, and my passion to serve God was renewed and stronger than ever before. God also provided my first female mentor, who led our study. It had been a very dry four years, and my spirit was ready to soar. Through this Bible study, I met Heather and Lori, and we became the best of friends. Although we did not get to see a lot of each other, we met once a week at Starbucks to pray together.

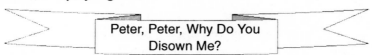

Peter, Peter, Why Do You Disown Me?

I became very involved in the ministries at Abundant Life Christian Fellowship led by Pastor Paul Sheppard. His teaching made me yearn for more of God. School was good, and by this time, I had decided that teaching biology to these kids was not the most important thing in life. I wanted to help them make real-life decisions. So I went back to school at night and during the summer and got my master's degree in school counseling. And the great news was that our school counselor was leaving, so there was an opening for me.

Counseling was very different from teaching. I missed the daily interaction with the kids, but I was able to help guide, direct, and encourage kids in more than just biology. I was able to help them with their college and life choices. I had to get used to not being in control of my day. As a teacher, I had every minute of my day planned out, but as a counselor at this school, I constantly put out fires and dealt with whatever walked through my door. God used me and taught me so much about the needs of these inner-city kids. I also played the role of school nurse, since we did not have one. As a biology teacher, everyone just figured I could help. One day, a young lady walked into my office and said she wasn't feeling well. I asked her if she wanted to call home, and she said she needed to call her doctor. Now this was not a typical response, so I recognized that there was more to this than I knew. After talking with her doctor, this student told me she needed to go to get her blood taken at another high school. I told her I would drive her, since her mom was not available and she would otherwise have had to take the bus. On the way there, I learned that she had leukemia. Who would have guessed? She was the star basketball player and the head cheerleader. She was very active and full of life.

On the way there, I asked her if she had some sort of faith to help her through, and she said no. I felt the Holy Spirit say, "You need to share with her." But I dropped her off and brushed away the pleas of the Holy Spirit. Soon after that, she was hospitalized at Stanford Hospital, and again I heard the Holy Spirit say, "You need to share with her." So I called her up and asked if it would be okay if someone from my church came to visit her. She said that would be nice, and

I began to make the arrangements, since the hospital was near my church and they had people who did hospital visitations. Again I heard the Holy Spirit say, "You need to share with her." Finally I called some people at the church personally to ask them to stop in and see her. Two days later, I received a call that this young lady had passed away.

The words of John 21:15-17 smacked me in the face:

> When they had finished eating, Jesus said to Simon Peter, "Simon, son of John, do you truly love me more than these?"

> "Yes, Lord," he said, "you know that I love you."

> Jesus said, "Feed my lambs."

> [16]Again Jesus said, "Simon, son of John, do you truly love me?"

> He answered, "Yes, Lord, you know that I love you."

> Jesus said, "Take care of my sheep."

> [17] The third time he said to him, "Simon, son of John, do you love me?" Peter was hurt because Jesus asked him the third time, "Do you love me?" He said, "Lord, you know all things; you know that I love you." Jesus said, "Feed my sheep."

Three times God told me to share with her, and three times I denied him. Lord, I will never hear Your call again and not do what You ask of me. From then on, my boldness in the school took on a whole new level.

CHAPTER 12

Careful What You Pray For

"I will give you a new heart and put a new spirit in you; I will remove from you your heart of stone and give you a heart of flesh" (Ezekiel 36:26). This became my prayer. I put so many layers around my heart to protect it that I wanted it to be set free. I shared this with my small group, Heather and Lori, that I wanted a new heart and asked them to pray this with me. I wanted to be able to give my heart away and trust God and a man with it, but my heart was hard.

Aug. 25, 2002

> *Lord, You are my strength. It has been a long time of spiritual dryness. Lord, my soul now longs to be quenched. A new school year is upon me—it's been over a year since Justin passed. I have grown in many ways over the past few years. My love for my family has grown—thank You for the family You placed me in. Father, I pray for all those students that will be in my classes this year. Lord, feed them physically, spiritually, paternally, and emotionally. Lord, help me to see them through Your eyes of compassion.*

Change is good but never easy. It usually means swallowing my pride and lying at the foot of the cross in surrender to Christ. A sermon I heard on finding God's best for a spouse for me made a lot of sense. There are three key attributes in a significant other that God will provide when it is the "right" one: Fabric—what is he made of? I can't change who he is, so he must be the type of man I desire and deserve. Fit—do our goals and passions fit together? Do we desire similar things? Finances—does he add to my spiritual account or does he only withdraw? This made sense, and I prayed that I could find such a man. I was tired of making excuses for men I had dated and defending some part of the relationship by saying, "Yes, but they have so much potential!"

Sept. 21, 2002

> *Lord, I want to love with Your love—not selfishly or hesitantly. Fill my heart with Your love so that it may overflow from within me. Lord, I pray for a fervent love, a sacred affection, a pure heart, and sensitivity to people's needs and a tender spirit.*

> *Father, thank You that Your love never fails. Living in San Francisco, I am faced with so much worldliness. Give me the knowledge to know when to rebuke and when to accept out of love. I feel that my own "morals and ethics" have been watered down, living here. I don't want that. May my love for the sinner grow ever stronger, but may my awareness of the sin be based on the truth of Scripture.*

> *This brings me to the next thing on my heart pertaining to love. Lord, I admit that I made a poor choice in my last relationship. You saved me! I feel like I know the type of man You want me to be with. Lord, one who loves You first and foremost, encourages and*

blesses my relationship with You, and, makes me feel like a princess. Lord, I want to be married to a man who loves You, loves kids, and loves me.

Lastly, I bring my job to You. Lord, I was unprepared for all the heartache and pain these youth are facing. This is where I need Your love, strength, and wisdom. Help me to serve each student as if I was serving You.

I really began to meditate on the verse, "Love the Lord your God with all of your heart, soul, mind, and strength." How do I do this?

Heart—Lord, thank You that You have given me a new heart, one capable of love. May my heart overflow with love so it affects my soul, mind, and strength. I cannot obtain that kind of love—it must come from You, Lord. I give my heart completely over to You, Jesus. May Your perfect love be made complete in my heart.

Soul—May I love You with all that I am. My innermost being. Pure and holy, with all of my soul—my very nature.

Mind—may all my thoughts and words be held captive by Your love. Lord, thank You for renewing my mind. Every day I must surrender this to You. This is where I need You the most, in loving You with my entire mind. My earthly experiences with love have not been born out of the type of love You require. May You teach me how to love You with my entire mind—all the time. If I love You with my entire mind, then I will trust You completely.

Strength—Lord, You have blessed me in so many ways. Lord, I am slowly learning that my strength is not sufficient. My strength leads to death, destruction, and disappointment. My strength has only allowed me to survive in the earthly realm. Lord, I need Your strength when it comes to giving You and loving You with all my heart, soul, and mind. Lord, if there are behaviors that I am doing that are taking my strength, please reveal those to me.

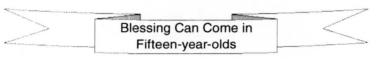

Blessing Can Come in
Fifteen-year-olds

After two years of living in Burlingame, life was good. My new apartment was closer to work, church, great shopping, restaurants, and running trails. Thing were fine until one day at church, I turned around, and there was my stalker! I went to the cops again and let the church know about him. He must have known where I lived and followed me to church, since my church was about sixty miles from where we used to live. It was not a coincidence. Before, when he was my neighbor, I thought he was just weird, but now I was afraid. I had to move again, because clearly he must have figured out that I had moved to Burlingame, and he was once again stalking me.

During this time, God had blessed me immensely, and I was able to buy a two-bedroom apartment in Foster City, California. I felt safe again, now that I was moving. It was about fifteen miles from my old apartment, in a very nice neighborhood overlooking the bay. It felt great to be a first-time homeowner, and I was able to decorate the way I wanted. There was a running/biking trail right across the street that ran along the shore of the bay. This place was perfect and peaceful! The first full day in my new house, I had just returned from a run and was stretching in the yard when a car pulled up very slowly. When I made eye contact with the driver, I realized it was my stalker. Our eyes locked before he drove off. I tried to make out his license plate number; then I ran inside and called the police. They ran the plate, and it matched my stalker, but they were unable to find him. I also followed up with the church, to let them know what had happened, and they banned him from attending any event there. They did offer him counseling, though.

We again had to go to court to get the restraining order renewed, since it had expired. Thankfully, Heather and her husband Jonathan went with me, as I did not want to go alone. I was very worried that the judge might believe *his* claim that I was stalking and following *him*. But the moment he opened his mouth, I realized that I did not have to worry, as it was evident that he was crazy. He was speaking nonsense about the Dallas Cowboys, and what that had to do with anything was beyond all of us. I also had a friend who was the assistant DA, and he found out that my stalker had other charges against him in another county and let the judge know this before issuing the sentence. The judge gave me the maximum six-year restraining order and told me to buy some mace, since he was crazy. The two arrest warrants out for him were in other counties, so there was nothing they could do. I never did see him again but still to this day look over my shoulder.

It was at this point that God began to place it on my heart to become a foster parent. I shared this with my prayer partners and Bible study group but never took any steps toward getting licensed. What did I, a single woman with very little free time on her hands, know about raising a child? Yet I felt that there was a reason I was blessed with a two-bedroom apartment, and that extra bedroom was to be used for God's glory.

Then, one morning when I got to work, one of my students, Jessica, sat on the ground next to my office door. She asked if she could talk to me. As she began to tell me her story I felt my heart stir in a way it had never stirred. She was fifteen years old and pregnant. She had lived with her mom and sister but had to move to a shelter after the pregnancy. Jessica's mom did not take the news that she was pregnant well, and it was no longer safe for the two of them to live under the same roof.

Without thinking, I asked her if she wanted to stay at my house for the weekend. I got a hold of her mom, and she agreed and wrote a letter of permission for her to be with me for that time. We spent the weekend talking about her options, and she eventually changed her mind about aborting the baby and decided to keep it. She even went to church with me and loved that. As I took her home that Sunday night, I told her to call me if things got bad at home, and I would come get her. And they did. Jessica called me that night from the hospital after getting into a fight with her mom. She was now in child protective custody until they could find a placement for her. It was then that I knew I had to take her in. She was the one to live in the extra bedroom that God gave me.

Because I had a previous relationship with Jessica, it was easy to get an emergency placement with Social Services. They deemed me "like family," so I didn't have to go through the hours of training prior to taking her in. She could move in immediately. It was agreed that she would live with me until the birth, and then they would find a new home for her with someone who could help with the baby. She came to live with me just after Thanksgiving 2004. I was determined to be a good "mom" to this young lady. I got up every morning to make her eggs and pack two lunches, in case she got hungry during the day. Luckily, I was a morning person. She, however, was a pregnant teenager, and waking up in the morning was the last thing she wanted. For the remainder of that semester, she attended our school and then transferred to a school for teen moms. It worked out well, but there were still areas where we really struggled. She was convinced that she loved her baby's dad, and I was convinced that he should be arrested for rape. The age difference was about ten years. This was one area where her mother and I agreed.

One Sunday at church, just after the sermon, Pastor Paul asked if anyone wanted to come up and accept Jesus as their personal savior. I told Jessica that if she did, I would walk up there with her. She said she wanted to, and that day, she gave her life to Jesus. We spent each night after that discussing Scripture, God's love, her family, and her gifts and talents. Jessica's social worker had agreed to pay for her plane ticket so that she could go to Colorado with me for Christmas break. I was very excited about showing her what a healthy, Christ-centered Christmas holiday looks like; no fighting or back-stabbing, just love and joy.

I had planned a lot of great activities for our trip. I should have seen the writing on the wall when we landed and the temperature was five degrees below zero, by far the coldest temperature Jessica had ever been in. We spent a few nights in Vail, Colorado, so she could see that beautiful city. Both of my sisters-in-law were there and pregnant, so the three of them could really bond. Then we went to my parents' house for Christmas, where my family doted on her and lavished her with gifts. Then, for New Year's Eve, we went to my aunt and uncle's in Denver. All my cousins and their kids joined us, totaling about twenty-five people. But something unexpected happened. It was too overwhelming for her. All the love and family was just too much, and she just wanted to stay in her room. She was miserable. My heart broke for her. I remember her stories of staying in the park when her mom was on drugs and her dad was in prison. How she had to take care of her sister in the Tenderloin, one of the roughest neighborhood in San Francisco. Oh, God, why wasn't I sensitive to this?

When we got back, she started at her new school, where they taught her about being a mom, along with her core subjects. One Sunday, she invited her mom to join us at church, and she came. When it came time for the altar call at the end of the service, Jessica grabbed her mom's hand, and the two of them walked up there as her mom gave her life to Christ. What a glorious day that was! I was very excited for Jessica and her mom. In fact, a few weeks later, as we were talking about that moment, I asked her what she had said to her mom when they went up. She looked at me and said, "I told her that we were going up there to give her life to Christ, just like you did to me!" I was in shock. I did not *say* to her that we were going up. I gently *asked* her if she wanted to go up, and if she did, I would join her. Jessica was very adamant that I told her she was going up; otherwise she would have been too scared to do it. We started laughing hysterically. I thought I said one thing, yet she heard something else. Only God could do something like that.

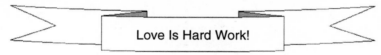

Love Is Hard Work!

Jessica's new school was a blessing and a curse. She was very much in love with her baby's dad, and every chance she got, she would skip school to see him. I could not keep tabs on her now that she was not at my school. We started arguing about her skipping school, her seeing him, and not being honest with me. These were typical teenage daughter/mother things, but it was all new to me. I lived far south of the city, so she was not able to visit her boyfriend, friends, or mom unless I took her to the train. This dependence on me was very hard, but it showed me that I have what it takes to love selflessly.

"I will give you a new heart and put a new spirit in you; I will remove from you your heart of stone and give you a heart of flesh" (Ezekiel 36:26). Lord, I see You pulling the layers of protection away from my heart. Lord, help me to trust You to protect my heart so I don't have to. I see how much Jessica loves her mom and dad, even though they were abusive and they abandoned her. I can learn a lot from her love.

Jessica would come with me to my Bible study group and end up just sleeping in the bedroom. The entire group began to take responsibility for raising her. Robbie, our leader, just loved on her. Mosella, who is a doula (birthing coach), met with her once a week to go over the birthing process and would cook some good soul food. Jimmy bought her maternity outfits, and Heather and Lori prayed with her. Yes, Jessica even got up at 5:00 a.m. to join us at Starbucks to pray. She memorized her favorite verse: "Trust in the Lord with all your heart and lean not on your own understanding; in all your ways acknowledge him, and he will make your paths straight" (Proverbs 3:5-6). We had our "village" to help raise this young lady. This was truly an example of the body of Christ coming together to love a child of God.

"I pray that out of his glorious riches he may strengthen you with power through his Spirit in your inner being, so that Christ may dwell in your hearts through faith. And I pray that you, being rooted and established in love, may have power, together with all the saints, to grasp how wide and long and high and deep is the love of Christ and to know this love that surpasses knowledge—that you may be filled to the measure of all the fullness of God." (Ephesians 3:16-19)

Lord, how can I teach her about Your love and the depths of it if I can't grasp it myself? Help us both to grasp this love.

R & R in El Salvador

It was the middle of January, and Jessica had been living with me for two months. I was ready for a weekend break. Thankfully, I had a wedding to attend, and it was in El Salvador. Jeff Varick, my buddy from Zurich, was going to marry Deedee Drysdale, who comes from El Salvador. I wouldn't miss this wedding! We were able to find a woman in my church who was wonderful and had a foster-care license to take Jessica for the four days. All I wanted to do was lie by the pool and sleep. It was just what I needed.

I took the redeye flight and arrived early Friday morning, just in time to join the wedding group for a hike up a volcano. Unfortunately, I was not feeling well, and during the entire hike, I wanted to throw up. I was the weakest link on the hike, and that killed my pride. The only person behind me was the armed guard they hired to protect us. Everyone had to wait for me! It was a small destination wedding, mostly with couples. There were two single guys and one other single woman. Everyone hung out together, and it was nice.

Saturday morning, a group of us went shopping, and others stayed at the pool. After lunch, we all hung out at the pool, and I was very much looking forward to vegging out. It was not to be. The hotel was buzzing with activity because there was a huge TV fundraiser going on; all the famous Central and South American actors and singers stayed at our hotel. In fact, many of them were hanging out at the pool with us, including the group Menudo. It was hot out, and so after a few minutes of lying out, I sat at the edge of the pool and soaked my feet in the freezing water. It was very refreshing. Then, one of the wedding guests, David Bushi, came and sat next to me. We started talking and playing with Jeff's middle-school nieces. Four hours later, we said good-bye because I was totally fried and needed to get ready for the wedding.

During the wedding reception, I sat at a table with the groomsmen and pastor. I was a bit disappointed, because I had enjoyed talking to David earlier that day. When it came time for dessert, a waiter delivered a piece of carrot cake and coffee from "the gentleman over there"—he pointed at David. It was at that moment I realized that I was sort of drawn to him. Prior to this, I was so focused on Jessica and resting that I was not looking to meet anyone new, especially a man.

The next day, we all met up and drove ninety minutes to Deedee's aunt's beach house, where we spent the day. Again, they had armed guards with Uzis on the beach, to protect us while we cooked a pig. David and I spent the entire day together, walking on the beach, playing in the waves, and sitting in the hammocks. We had so much fun—he had an uncanny knack for getting me to talk a lot! I usually do the listening. We also had a ball, playing in the ocean, trying to body surf. The waves and current were so strong that several times David would be talking to me and turn around to see where I was, only to find me about a hundred meters down shore, swept away. That evening, we sat on the beach and watched the most awesome sunset I have ever seen.

That night, we all met in Jeff and Deedee's room to open gifts. Upon completion of that, we all said good-bye and good night. Deedee looked around the room, thanked us all for coming, and as she looked my way said, "We will all be together again at the next wedding." Thankfully, I was already sunburned, because I am sure my face went beet red. It was a very refreshing weekend, and a new spark ignited in my heart.

Jan. 31, 2005

My heart is so full of joy and love. The wedding in El Salvador was wonderful. Jeff and Deedee will serve the Kingdom well. Jessica did okay away with Betty. It's nice to see her again and hear her talk about sharing God's love with the other teen moms.

Most of all, I want to thank God for introducing me to David Bushi. He is everything I've ever looked for and so very much more. I am not sure if You brought him into my life to show me that there are wonderful, single men of God out there or have You sent him to me. I am trying not to read into the weekend and trust God with my heart. We didn't even exchange contact information, so God will have to spur David on, if that is His plan for us. I don't want to write too much, in fear that I will not hear from him again. His devotion to You, Lord, has struck such a chord with my heart and soul. Thank You, Lord, for sending him into my life, even if it was just for a weekend.

CHAPTER 13

Exceedingly Abundantly Beyond My Dreams

On April 25, 2005, Jessica gave birth to a healthy baby girl. I had the great privilege of being in the room with her when she delivered. It was such a special occasion. Even though her baby's dad, her mom, her doula, and I were all in there, we put aside our differences and loved this girl and her baby. Jessica and her baby had to stay in the hospital for a few days, because it was a high-risk pregnancy at her age. This gave the social worker time to find her a new placement, one where her foster parents could help her more with the baby than I could. I lived far from her school and the comfort zone of the city she grew up in, and I just felt she would be too isolated in my house. I wasn't ready to give up all my activities to help her with the baby like she deserved.

After three days Jessica and her baby were released from the hospital, only after the police took DNA samples from her, the baby, and her baby's dad, in order to prove he is the father when they arrested him for rape. I was back to work and thankful that Jessica and her daughter had found a new home and that both were healthy. It was a rainy day in San Francisco, and out of the blue, Jessica appeared at the door of my office, soaking wet. I shot up out of my desk chair and asked her what she was doing there. She told me she and her baby were released from the hospital today and had no way to get home, so they got in a cab. Then, when she got to her new home, the foster mother was not home and she had no way in. So she drove around in the cab and accumulated a fifty-dollar fare, until she thought to come see me. My heart just broke. I ran outside, and the baby was still in the cab. The secretaries and principal quickly came to my aid, and we collected enough money to pay the fare and bring them in out of the rain. I held her little baby that day in my office as tears rolled down my cheeks. What a way to start off your life as a new mom, no money and nowhere to go!

"For I know the plans I have for you, declares the Lord, plans to prosper you and not to harm you, plans to give you hope and a future" (Jeremiah 29:11). Oh, Lord, you must have great plans for Jessica and her baby girl!

Things did not get easier for Jessica after that. Her new foster home was in the government housing, also known as the projects, and she was afraid to even leave the safety of her four walls. She and her daughter were placed in different foster homes until she finally found a home with a good family who helped with her baby. Over the next year, we would still hang out and go to church together periodically. She had a new support system and was doing very well in school. She could take her baby to school with her, which was wonderful.

Colorado Calling!

In the spring of 2006, after six years in San Francisco, and three nieces and one nephew later, I decided it was time to move closer to my family so I could be a good aunt. I started to look for counseling jobs in Denver. David and I had talked a lot over the phone, but we remained just friends. I had hoped for more, but the distance between California and Michigan, where he lived, was too great. I had grown to lean on him as someone I could vent to about Jessica. He was "safe," because he was so far away. And once again, I had a good male friend—full stop. I was disappointed but thought perhaps I would meet a man like him in Denver. After all, that is not far from Colorado Springs, also known as Vatican II, with all the Christian organizations based there. I struggled, as always, with this decision to move or not. I loved my job, the school, my church, and my friends. I was very happy.

But then God moved. One day, out of the blue, David called and said that he felt strongly that I should move to Colorado. He didn't know why, but he thought that is what God had told him. That was the confirmation I needed, so I put my house up for sale and six days later had an offer for $5,000 above my asking price. I guess God was in the move. I was so sad about leaving my Bible study group and prayer partners. For the last four years, we had met weekly at Starbucks to pray. We prayed through two births, bouts with depression, breakups, fostering a teen mom, and sickness. This group of three dedicated prayer partners would be splitting geographically, but the distance would not weaken the bond we had. Heather wrote a good-bye poem that beautifully summed up our relationship:

Three Women
There are three women
One is a teacher, one is a mother and then there is the
youngest
They come from different places and testify to
different pasts
They take their coffee differently
Black, decaf when pregnant and iced
The three women have the same Father

Together they praise Him
Together they petition Him
Together they wait for His reply

There are two women
The mother and the youngest
The teacher has gone
Now they will take their coffee without her
Decaf when pregnant and iced

I, the Father see three women
One is a teacher, one is a mother and one is the
youngest
The teacher is not with them
Can you hear them praise me in union?
They wait for my reply
And I answer my daughters, "A cord of three strands is
not quickly broken."

Ecclesiastes 4:12

I wasn't able to find a counseling job but got a job with a nonprofit called Whiz Kids Tutoring. It seemed like a perfect fit, as I would be training volunteers to tutor homeless kids as part of the mayor's initiative to end homelessness. After working with Jessica, I had definitely developed a heart for homeless kids, and this was a perfect fit. I loaded up a truck, and with the help of my dad and a couple of friends, we all drove from California to Colorado. I stayed with my aunt and uncle while I looked for a place to buy.

During all of this, one of my good friends from church, Santosh Poonen, had proposed to a gal, and they were getting married just outside of Detroit, Michigan. This was the perfect opportunity to see David again. I invited him to escort me to the wedding and he agreed. He had arranged for me to stay at the house of his best friend and his family, which was very nice.

We had a great time at the Poonen wedding, and the weather was perfect. It was held at a retreat center, around a lake. It was an outdoor wedding, and the presence of God was very powerful. Once again, just like it was almost two years ago, the conversation between David and me flowed very easily. I really wished that we lived in the same state so we could see if this friendship would develop into dating. He was adamantly against long-distance dating, and that is all I had really known—there was safety in that. So, after the wedding, we said good-bye and went our separate ways.

I started my new job and was busy with that and trying to get plugged into a new church and leading a twenty-something women's Bible study. My phone conversations with Dave started to pick up after our meeting in Detroit. We started to talk most days, and some conversations went on for hours. Whiz Kids and the organization that runs them had an annual retreat in Vail, Colorado, every year. I took a chance and invited David to join us (about fifty people) on the retreat. To my surprise, he agreed and flew out the first part of October.

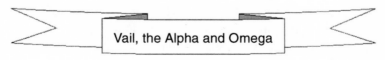

Vail, the Alpha and Omega

The Vail retreat was great. David and I had a good time getting to know each other even more. After the morning sessions on Saturday, we spent the day walking around Vail and shopping. After dinner, we had an evening praise session that everyone went to, and then we went on a walk together. It was pretty cold outside in the fall mountain air, but still we walked and walked. We found a path near the hotel that contained about a quarter-mile loop, and so we circled. Finally, he asked if I wanted to sit on a large rock, and we did. As we were sitting there, freezing our butts off, David asked me how I felt about him and shared how he felt about me. It was there on that rock that we decided to date.

I was in total shock. A man I thought was amazing but had somehow categorized in my mind as out of my league now wanted to date me. We got up hand in hand and started walking again. We walked and walked around and around the quarter-mile loop, completely frozen but not wanting to go inside or lose the moment. Finally we did go inside, and when I laid my head down on my pillow that night, I didn't want to sleep, so afraid was I that when I woke up, he would change his mind.

The next morning, we had to get up early in order to get him to the Denver airport in time to catch his flight. We were able to meet up with my nonna at church before the flight so she could meet him. She instantly fell in love with him too.

Oct. 18, 2006

"God will do exceedingly abundantly above all that we ask or imagine" (Eph. 3:20).

I sit here today in my new house in Lone Tree, Colorado, reflecting on the past several years. God has been so good, faithful, and blessed me in so very many ways. He's taken me from an insecure, proud, self-seeking girl all the way around the world and turned me into a woman who wants nothing more than to bathe in the light of Jesus. For all this I am so very thankful that He has taken my heart of stone and given me a heart of flesh.

God has given me the greatest gift my heart has ever longed for. In addition to finally allowing myself to feel His unconditional love—He has blessed me with a man here on Earth. A man after God's own heart. David is fully committed to serving God, and he thinks the world of me. My heart is so full of joy and love that words cannot express how I am feeling. I just lift up my heart and soul in thanks and praise. Hallelujah!

At 5:00 p.m., the most beautiful arrangement of twelve red roses arrived from David, aka The Man. I have never felt so loved by another human being. I am so excited to get to know this romantic side of him; I could live the rest of my life happy from this one gift—it came from his heart to mine.

Oct. 20, 2006

Praise God! I praise You, Lord, for Your faithfulness, for caring about all the details in my life. Lord, I praise You for the joy that is so deep I my soul. Lord, may this not be just a passing emotion but the closer Dave and I grow together and the closer we grow to You as a couple, may this joy grow as well.

Father, I commit our relationship to You, as Your fingerprints are all over it. Give us direction, Lord, and may we not be bound by "norms" and worldly expectations but directed by Your heavenly hands. "Love cannot be forced; love cannot be coaxed and teased. It comes out of heaven, unasked and unsought." —Pearl Buck

"Delight yourself in the Lord and He will give you the desires of your heart" (Psalm 37:4). Dave and I somehow managed to spend the next three out of four weekends together. Thank goodness for frequent-flier programs. He was even able to join me for a wedding back in the San Francisco Bay Area so that he could meet all my friends from there. Heather and Lori, who had faithfully prayed for this relationship, were very happy to meet him and see us together. We even had our first kiss on the Golden Gate Bridge. This relationship was turning into a fairy tale, and I was the princess. For the first time in my life, I felt valued, cherished, and loved, and the great part was that I could totally be myself!

Oct. 24, 2006

"Who hopes for what they already have? But if we hope for what we do not yet have we wait for it patiently" (Rom. 8:24-25).

Thank You, Lord, that You teach me patience in things that I hope for. For in waiting, it gives my heart time to align with my heavenly Father's. Lord, I thank You for giving me the desires of my heart—now that my desires are in unison with Your desires. I know that there is a reason David and I are apart for the next few months. Lord, may we both be teachable, patient, and put our hope in You. Lord, fill us with Your love so that we may love each other with that holy, godly, faithful kind of love so foreign to this world. Lord, Your way, timing, plans are perfect. I thank You and praise You.

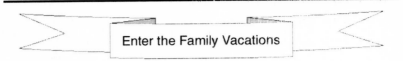

Enter the Family Vacations

For the first time in my life, I was in a healthy, godly relationship, and it was very freeing. I was actually proud to introduce him to my family, instead of trying to make excuses for him. I joined his family for Thanksgiving that year, at which time I met his parents and older brother and sister. Then he joined my family just after Christmas in Vail for a week of skiing and New Year's Eve. It was great, and we get along very well. I had a moment of freaking out while in Vail, where I was freezing up around him and had serious thoughts of ending the relationship. But then I looked deep into my heart and realized that I was scared because he was perfect, and after thirty-five years of waiting, I wasn't sure I was ready for this kind of relationship.

His family invited me to join them for their annual family vacation to Maui, Hawaii, in February. I was very excited but nervous about our first family vacation together. In my opinion, it was a fabulous trip. David and I would run together in the morning, come back home, and then the rest of his family would join us at the local public pool to swim laps. Then we returned to the condo for a fabulous brunch, followed by playing in the ocean all afternoon. Most nights, we just cooked in the condo, but David and I did sneak out on Valentine's Day for a very romantic dinner at the Lahina Fish Company. Every night we watched the sunset, and this became our favorite part of the day. Dave even went with me on a day trip to Kauai to visit an old family friend who was battling cancer. That spoke very deeply to my heart about what kind of man he was.

Things were going great, or so I thought. Because of both our jobs, we were unable to see each other until Easter. That was a very long couple of months. I flew up to Detroit to celebrate our Lord's resurrection with him, and his family drove up from Ohio. We had a nice time and started planning the next time we would be together. The weeks went by, and then I got the phone call that I had feared deep down inside would come because he was too good to be true. Dave said that it was just too hard with the distance and wasn't sure he ever wanted to get married. I could hardly speak, as I did not see it coming at all. I tried very hard to convince him that we were perfect together and that he was just afraid of change.

May 4, 2007

Oh Lord, my soul cries out in pain. I am devastated on all sides. Why is this happening? Why has a gift so clearly given by You been taken from me? Why has David chosen to turn from me? Lord, why is he not able to love? Lord, I know You can change a heart of stone into a heart of flesh that is able to love. Lord, I beg You to do this for Dave.

Father, at times the pain is unbearable and seems to be getting worse. Lord, we are so perfect together. I don't understand! Lord, I trust You are in control, but the pain and loneliness are so great—my heart hurts and cannot find joy at the moment. Holy Spirit, please, I beg of You to fill Dave's heart with a love so great that it overflows. Tear down those walls that have been built up. I will not give up on him, Lord, unless You clearly tell me to. He is Your beloved; You will not leave him where he is. Oh Lord, wrap Your arms around me right now and take some of this pain from me. I feel like I have suffered a death. I long to be with You in Your kingdom. Lord, I don't understand. All I can do is trust that You are still working this love out in both of us and will bring us back together.

Father, Holy Spirit, give me wisdom and discernment. I want so badly to be in contact with him. Lord, what should I do? Lord, rock his world with love. Take away his fear of intimacy and fill him with Your abounding, consuming, reckless love. Lord, I will not cease in praying for his heart!

Lord, search my heart, even the broken pieces and the gaping hole, test me and know my anxious thoughts. See if there is any offensive way in me and lead me in the way everlasting.

I had to cling to the Word, because that was all I could hold on to. God comforted me with a word from Psalm 147:3, 5, and 11. "He heals the brokenhearted and binds up their wounds." Lord, please just stop the bleeding. Can You, and will You, really bind my wound that is so deep? "His understanding has no limits." Thank You for the understanding, because no one else in this world can understand the pain I have. "The Lord delights in those who fear him, who put their hope in his unfailing love." Lord, You are my only hope right now. I need You, even to take my next breath.

After three days of fasting, praying, and seeking God, He has met me in a painful way. God's Word in Isaiah says after a fast, your healing will quickly appear. "Then your light will break forth like the dawn, and your healing will quickly appear; then your righteousness will go before you, and the glory of the Lord will be your rear guard" (Isaiah 58:8). I still feel like the bleeding hasn't stopped. Today would have been Justin's thirty-ninth birthday, and I miss him so much. He would understand my pain and sadness.

May 29, 2007

I know God says He will never leave me nor forsake me, and this I cling to, because I feel so forsaken by Dave. He had all the love I was capable of, all my trust and it wasn't enough for him. I feel that he has rejected me not because of his own fears or inabilities but because I am not enough. I fear I will never be able to love a man again out of fear of rejections.

However, it was through this fasting process that God has done two significant things: One, He showed me once again that He has called me to help and serve the poor and homeless. I stopped doing that this year, even though it was my job. My heart was not where it needed to be. And two, God very painfully showed me how selfish I had become. The motivation behind my actions this past year was very selfish. You can do what looks good. Holy in the eyes of those around you but my motive was not to honor God but uplift Angie.

Instead of building David up and encouraging him in his faith and ministries, I pulled him from those. We first became interested in each other when we were both involved in active service. Once we started dating, that stopped. I ignored the Lord time and time again. He spoke to my heart about this, and I kept praying for Dave to take the lead. God wasn't telling me to be still and let Dave lead; here He was asking me to and I didn't.

1 Timothy 6:6 says, "But godliness with contentment is great gain." I have not been content with God; my desire to be loved by a man has become stronger than my contentment. I cannot honestly say, You, Lord, are all I seek and God is all I want. I have listened to the world and the message that only in marriage are you truly a princess. And my desire for a family has become greater than my desire to honor God. I can't in all honesty ask God to take away this desire either.

I have never experienced such loneliness as I have these past six weeks. I never felt such a part of something and so connected to someone, only to have it yanked from me. What a void there is in my life. I wish Dave would do something to make me realize that he's not the man I thought he was or do something for me to see how wrong we were. But as it stands, I still believe he is the wonderful man of God that God wanted me to walk through this life with. I will not give up praying for Dave to change his mind. He is the one for me, and God has such great plans for us together. Please, Holy Spirit, help him to not be controlled by fear or being "safe" but help him to step out in faith.

If God created me/woman to be a helper and encourager, it's no wonder why Dave wouldn't want to be with me when I did not encourage him in the Lord. I was more of a detractor. Oh God, forgive me!

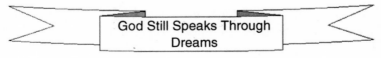

God Still Speaks Through Dreams

Every time I stepped away from working in a school, it seemed like God pulled me back. The grant that covered my Whiz Kids job was ending, and so I once again found a job in a Denver public high school as a counselor. Lucky for me, a counselor at John F. Kennedy High

School just got married and was taking a seven-month sabbatical to travel the world with his new wife. So I stepped in for the second semester of school starting in January, and it was a great fit.

It has been months since Dave and I broke up. God spoke to me; otherwise I would never have been able to let him go. It's so hard to understand, because we got along so well and loved each other so much. But God spoke very clearly to me in a dream, and I must obey.

Saturday night, I had a dream that I bought a new house. Three significant women in my life, my mom, Barb Bowman my former Young Life leader, and her daughter Annalise, were helping me to decorate and re-arrange furniture. Barb pointed to a door and asked where it went. I didn't know what it led to, and when we opened it, it was the most amazing room in the house. I didn't even know it was there when I bought the house. Then, while we arranged that room, we opened another door, which led to an amazing greenhouse that I didn't know was there. I woke up and felt that God was telling me that He was going to open many doors that led to amazing things. So I waited, patiently optimistic and full of hope that God had great plans for my life.

Then, the next day after church, I went for a prayer walk/run to pray for direction with Dave and our relationship. All of a sudden, I was stopped in my tracks, and a very clear vision came to me. Dave was in a small rowboat out on a lake, and Jesus was asking him to step out of the boat. God told him that he was very good at being in the boat and would be safe, secure, and provided for in the boat. In fact, he was admired by some for his skills in the boat. But Jesus was asking him to step out of the boat. David was actually trapped in the boat and living no life at all compared to what God had planned for him, and he would not be free to live and love until he stepped out.

I watched from a distance and tried to encourage Dave that he was the greatest "boat person" ever. Jesus looked at me and told me I had to step out of Dave's life so that God could have his heart. I was being a crutch or hindrance to Dave hearing God. God asked me to let Dave go, so He could do what it takes to get him to step out of the boat. To show my love for Dave and obedience to God, I had to let him go. Thinking about the dream I had the night before, it was clear to me that God was speaking directly to me about the great things that await me. He has great plans for Dave as well, but we needed to let go of our relationship in order to allow God to work in our hearts and lives. Meanwhile, unbeknownst to me, that very day God told Dave he needed to let me go because it wasn't fair to keep me hanging on.

I loved him very much and missed his friendship. There was a big hole in my life now, but the pain of a broken heart was minimized because I was faithful to God and let Dave go. To cling to this relationship at this point would be in direct disobedience to God. I prayed continually that God would do whatever was necessary to get Dave's faith to go from his head to his heart, because I felt he was afraid of change and of loving. I prayed that Dave would become passionate about loving and serving God, and that if the Lord sees fit, He will bring Dave back to me, ready, willing, and able to love as God created him to love. Lord, hear my cries and prayers. "During the days of Jesus's life on earth, he offered up prayers and petitions with loud cries and tears to the one who could save him from death, and he was heard because of his reverent submission" (Hebrews 5:7).

Bears on the bus in Bulgaria

Easter in Israel

ROMANIA '96

Project

Service Project to a Romania orphanage

Masato and I enjoying sushi

Christmas in Kenya

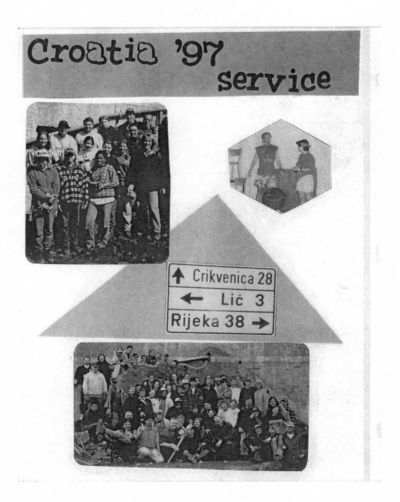

Croatia '97 service

Crikvenica 28
← Lič 3
Rijeka 38 →

Service Project to a Croatian Refugee housing

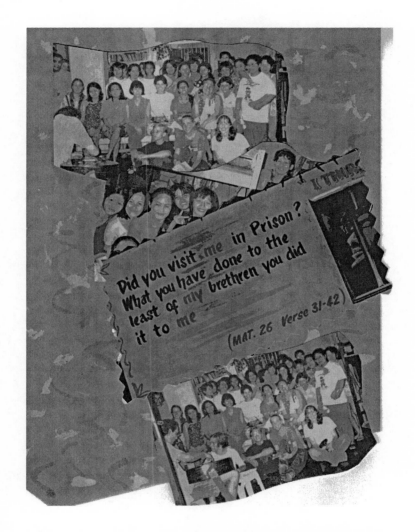

Singing and visiting with the women in prison in the Phillippines

Monthly visits to a Philippines Men's Prison

My engagement to David in Vail, CO

Angie, Jessica and baby Neveah

Our wedding with kids singing Jesus Loves Me

CHAPTER 14

From a Feather to a Bushi

I started getting more involved at work and found a community of
friends there. Business was picking up, and this helped in getting
over Dave. I wrote a letter to him but never mailed it. I needed to put
some thoughts and prayers on paper, but e-mail was too risky, as I
might actually send it to him.

> *Dave,*
>
> *I keep asking that the God of our Lord Jesus Christ,
> the glorious Father, may give you the spirit of wisdom
> and revelation, so that you may know Him better. I pray
> also that the eyes of your heart may be enlightened in
> order that you may know the hope to which He has called
> you, the riches of His glorious inheritance in the saints,
> and His incomparably great power for us who believe
> (Eph 1:17-19).*
>
> *"I pray that out of His glorious riches He may
> strengthen you with power through His Spirit in your
> inner being, so that Christ may dwell in your hearts
> through faith. And I pray that you, being rooted and
> established in love, may have power, together with all
> the saints, to grasp how wide and long and high and*

*deep is the love of Christ and to know this love surpasses
knowledge" (Eph. 3:16-19).*

*I know God is transforming your heart to receive
and give His love abundantly. "If two of you on earth
agree about anything you ask for, it will be done for you
by my father in heaven" (Matt. 18:19). God, give Dave
and Angie Your peace and blessing for marriage. It is in
Your name we pray.*

Dave and I had been in touch a few times, and to my surprise
he asked if he could come out in late September; he wanted to go
to Vail. So we did and had a great time. He flew in Friday night,
and we drove to Vail. Saturday morning, we went to Lion's Head
in Vail, at the base of the gondola, and began the long hike up the
mountain. It was a glorious fall day, and the sun was shining; it was
God's creation at its best. It took most of the morning to hike up,
and then we sat down at the top of Lion's Head and soaked up the
sun. We realized how much we enjoy being together, and I could feel
this hopefulness inside of me well up again. All that hard work of
trying to get over him was gone, and I was still very much in love
with him. We rode the gondola down the mountain and then found
a nice patch of grass to lie down in. We lay there watching people
and dogs go by. It was Oktoberfest, so a lot of interesting characters
in lederhosen kept walking by. Finally, after a nap on the grass, we
walked into the town to join in the festivities. It was the perfect day,
topped off with Italian gelato. That night, we went to the Red Lion
restaurant in downtown Vail to eat. Every time we went to Vail, we
ate at the Red Lion, so it had become our spot.

Sunday morning, we left early for Denver so that we could go
to my church, have brunch, and then go to the airport. I think out of
the hundreds of times we'd said good-bye at the airport, this was the

hardest for me. How could I let the guard around my heart down so easily and quickly? But there was something different about Dave's heart this time. Could it be that God had heard my prayers and taken away his fear? Angie, don't get your hopes up.

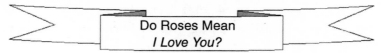

Do Roses Mean *I Love You?*

On Thursday October 2, 2008, I received a call from the secretary in the main office that a package had been delivered for me. I had been waiting for a few online exams to arrive, so I went downstairs to her office to pick them up. As I approached the main office, a number of other teachers stood around the secretary's desk, and when they saw me, they broke out in smiles. As they parted, I saw a dozen long-stemmed red roses in a beautiful vase. Dave had sent me roses. I didn't even know that he knew the name of the school where I worked. There was no special occasion for the flowers, so I was very surprised. I called to thank him, and he asked if he could come again this weekend. I was so excited, yet I tried not to allow my heart to get too involved. I called him immediately and thanked him very much. I brought them back to my office, where all the female faculty members would keep coming in to see them.

The next day was Friday, and Dave was to fly in around 5:00 p.m. I tried very hard to focus on my work and not think about him. Then I got a call from the secretary again to tell me that I had another "package" in the main office. I ran downstairs and saw another dozen long-stemmed roses. Oh my gosh! What was happening? Now the ladies in the office wanted to know what was going on, and I told them I had no idea. Again I took them upstairs and called Dave immediately to thank him. He was already on his way to the airport. He said he wanted me to feel like a princess, and I did. I had never received flowers at work before, but now, two days in a row, I got roses.

Those four hours I had to wait until it was time to go pick him up at the airport were the longest of my life. I even ran home first and changed out of my work clothes into something cute for him. I actually had butterflies in my stomach because I was so excited. When I saw him come up out of the tram, I ran to him and jumped into his arms to thank him for the flowers. I just about knocked him over. The surprises didn't stop there. As soon as we got back to my house, he presented me with three gorgeous outfits from Ann Taylor—my favorite store! Apparently, he had all the ladies at Ann Taylor in tears when he told them that he was buy these outfits to surprise me. I had such a hard time sleeping that night, as all I could think about was how amazing Dave was and how for the first time in my life, I felt pursued.

Saturday morning, October 4, 2008, we once again drove to Vail for the afternoon. The trees were changing colors into brilliant golds and oranges. As we pulled into a parking spot, it began to sprinkle rain. We grabbed the large golf umbrella that I had in the car and headed out for a walk. The next thing I knew, we were on the trail where we first started to date two years ago. We headed toward "our rock" where we initially decided to date, but because of the rain, it was too wet to sit down on it.

At this point, we stopped walking, and standing face-to-face under the umbrella, Dave began to share from his heart. He said that from the moment we met, we felt like best friends. He said that he knows he was hard on me, but I never gave up, and loved him unconditionally. He said some more amazing things, but at this point, my mind could not absorb it all, because it felt like a dream. Then he handed me the umbrella and he dropped to his knee. He began, "Angie Feather, I love you. Will you marry me?" As soon as he dropped to his knees, I began to cry and could hardly answer him.

Here, in one moment in time, at the age of thirty-seven, a man who stood for everything I ever prayed for was asking me to be his wife. God heard my heart all these years and prepared the two of us for each other. After I gathered myself and stopped crying, we called both our families to tell them the great news. We spent a few more hours in Vail, where we walked and basked in the moment. By the time we hopped back in the car to drive home, my cheeks hurt from all the smiling I did.

"Trust in the Lord with all your heart, lean not on your own understandings, in all your ways acknowledge him and he will make your path straight." Proverbs 3:5&6.

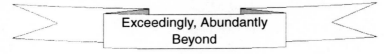

Exceedingly, Abundantly Beyond

"God will do exceedingly, abundantly beyond what you hope or imagine" (Eph. 3:20, American Standard Version). This had been my prayer for so long, and now I was marrying my Ephesians 3:20 man. I have to be honest and admit that since I had started dating Dave, I thought a lot about where I wanted to get married and have the reception. So I made a few phone calls on the drive back to Denver, and we had an appointment at a church in the mountains outside of Golden, Colorado and on Sunday afternoon, a meeting with the wedding planner at the Hyatt downtown Denver. My parents were very excited and even cut their trip short in Kansas visiting Luke and drove to Denver on Sunday to meet up with Dave and me at the potential reception site.

My nonna flew in from Pennsylvania that morning, so Dave and I went to the airport to surprise her. I think next to me, Nonna loved him more than anyone. I was supposed to meet her at the gate, and Dave was waiting at baggage claim for us. Our plan was not to tell her until we arrived at the reception site. Well, the plan didn't work out so well, because by the time I got through security and to her gate, the plane had already landed and she was taken by wheelchair to baggage claim. I started calling her cell phone, but she did not have it on, and Dave had left his in the car. I turned around and ran as fast as I could back through the terminal to baggage claim. When I arrived, I saw her standing hand-in-hand with Dave. Apparently he saw them wheeling her to baggage claim and followed them. As she stood there waiting for her luggage, he stood behind her and quietly said, "Hello, Nonna."

She turned around and with a shocked look on her face asked, "Are you here for business?" Dave said that he was not and that he was here to see me. She was very excited, and by the time I got to them, he had told her that he proposed. My Italian grandmother started screaming and crying. I had to tell everyone looking at us that we had just gotten engaged and that she was happy.

The three of us drove to downtown Denver and met up with my parents and the wedding planner. The venue was absolutely perfect, set on the thirty-fifth floor in downtown Denver, with all glass walls and a 360-degree view. It was very classy and spectacular. In what has to be all thanks to God, both the church and reception venue had availability on December 21, 2008! So there it was, only two and a half months away. Dave asked if I could plan a wedding in such a short time, and in unison, my mom, grandmother, and I said, "Yes!"

The next few months flew by with bridal showers, finding dresses, and making arrangements. In fact, the first weekend after my engagement, Stacy drove in from Kansas with Mom and baby in tow. Maria and my mom came in from Grand Junction, Colorado, and in one day, we found my wedding dress, their matron of honor dresses, and the two flower girl dresses. Again, a sign that God was in this marriage. Also during this engagement period, Dave began to lavish me with love and gifts. He allowed his changed heart to fully express the love it had inside. At this point, it was clear to me that he loved me every bit as much as I loved him. He loved me with a love that only God could give a forty-three-year-old bachelor who has never been married. I had Maria and Stacy—both of my sisters-in-law—as matrons of honor, and Dave had his brother Paul and best friend Ara. It was the biggest blessing to have Justin's daughter, Anaya, who was now seven years old, and Luke's oldest daughter, Annabelle, who was three years old, as our flower girls. That meant the world to me, to have all of them be a part of this special day that no one ever thought would come.

The day was a brilliant, sunny, yet cold day in Colorado. The church was in Golden, with a view of the mountains on all sides. As we said our vows and looked out the windows facing us, the sun began to set with another brilliant sunset. The sunset had become such a symbol of our relationship and God's glory to us. Because there are so many special young kids in our lives and only a few could be in the wedding, we had all eighteen of them join us on stage for a singing of "Jesus Loves Me," and it was beautiful. We wanted to make it very evident in the service that God would be honored. J.C. Bowman, my former Young Life leader, who was so significant in my life, honored us by officiating the ceremony and led us in our vows:

> *I, Angela, take you, David, to be my wedded husband. I believe in you, David. I want to help make all your dreams come true. I have seen your love for God, and I promise to support your decision and submit to your leadership, knowing you always seek God's will. I promise to be faithful, and I will never leave you. You*

are my best friend. I will pray for you daily, and I will always seek to grow closer to God. My desire is to be the woman you need me to be, your helper and encourager. I will make our home a place of rest, and I will always be there for you. I do promise and covenant before God and these witnesses to be your loving and faithful wife; in plenty and in want, in joy and in sorrow, in sickness and in health, as long as we both shall live.

I, David, take you, Angela, to be my wedded wife. I believe in you, Angie. I want to help make all your dreams come true. I have seen your love for God, and I promise to support your decisions and ministries. My arms will always be open to hold, comfort, and keep you safe as long as I am here on this earth. I will be your spiritual leader. I will keep Christ at the center of our relationship, so that we will have spirit-filled lives. I do promise and covenant before God and these witnesses to be your loving and faithful husband; in plenty and in want, in joy and in sorrow, in sickness and in health, as long as we both shall live.

The reception was everything we hoped it would be and more. On December 23, we left for our two-week honeymoon in Maui, where we celebrated our first Christmas and New Year together. It was the perfect ending to that chapter of my life and a great beginning for the next.

EPILOGUE

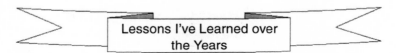

Lessons I've Learned over the Years

I want your prayer to be that God will provide exceedingly abundantly above all that you hope or imagine. I want your life to be desperate for Jesus and your heart open to love. I hope the lessons I have learned in my life will be a source of hope and encouragement for you.

- If I had known that God would bring someone like Dave into my life at age thirty-seven, it would have saved me a lot of tears and stress over the years. Imagine how different my life would have been if only I had lived a life that trusted that God would bring the perfect man to me instead of fretting so much.

- God heard my prayers over the years. I wanted a man who loved God and would be the leader of our house spiritually. I wanted him to be handsome, tall, and athletic. God said, *I will give you all that and exceeding abundantly more.* Dave is an amazing man of God, not just handsome but gorgeous. He can actually beat me in all sports except golf, is extremely smart, and we think so much alike that we never have conflict. Oh, how willing I was to settle early on and so thankful that God would not let me. But it took thirty-seven years for both of us to get to this point. Be specific when you pray about what you want. God will take any desires that are not in your best interest away from you if you are surrendering to Him.

- When your friends and family don't like the guy you are dating or if you stop doing the Bible studies and going to church, then you need to break off the relationship. This is not God's best for you. Much easier said than done. Stop making excuses for the guys you date. Remember, if you think that he will change once you marry him, you are wrong. The right relationship should not be so hard.

- I deserve to be a princess. It is so worth the wait to find the right man. Even though I felt like the old maid, I would rather wait thirty-seven years before I got married and live sixty-three years happily married than marry at twenty-five and have seventy-five years of struggles and unhappiness.

- Do not give up on your dreams. God took me around the world and provided many adventures. I never dreamed that big, but despite the hard times, I would not change any of it, because it was the adventure of a lifetime. You can serve God with all your heart and follow His leading and still desire to be married. God created us women to be man's helper, and He placed that longing in you to be married. Don't try to squash that desire in order to serve God. You can have and deserve both.

- Your mission field is where ever God has you at the moment. However, sometimes you need to step out of your comfort zone, get a little ruffled in order to grow into becoming that person God created you to be. God will work on both of you so that you are ready to meet in His timing when He knows you are ready. Again, trusting God's timing is so hard.

- Independence is good but stubbornness can be detrimental. Allow yourself to need and desire relationships with people. It's okay! Actually it's more than okay it's the way God made you!

- God will use you to further His kingdom, no matter where you live or how prepared or qualified you feel if you want to be used. Trust God with your heart to nurture, grow, and protect it.

- I now have two precious boys and drive a mini-van.

CPSIA information can be obtained
at www.ICGtesting.com
Printed in the USA
FSOW01n0027131215
14163FS